DATE DUE

HOW DO THEY GET RID OF IT?

HOW DO THEY
GET RID OF IT?

by
SUZANNE HILTON

THE WESTMINSTER PRESS

Philadelphia

STANDARD BOOK NO. 664–32462–2

LIBRARY OF CONGRESS CATALOG CARD NO. 70–94771

BOOK DESIGN BY
DOROTHY ALDEN SMITH

PUBLISHED BY THE WESTMINSTER PRESS®
PHILADELPHIA, PENNSYLVANIA

PRINTED IN THE UNITED STATES OF AMERICA

To make us love our country,
  our country ought to be lovely.
        —*Edmund Burke*

CONTENTS

INTRODUCTION

MAN IS A MAKER OF THINGS and a born collector. That is why this book had to be written. He has made and collected too much.

One year's trash from New York City would make a mile-high mountain in the middle of Yankee Stadium. The trash from Los Angeles would fill the Panama Canal in a year. Cincinnati, Ohio, would like to send its trash to Kentucky. Chicago, Illinois, wants to send its to Wisconsin.

Finally the clamor of worried citizens, upset congressmen, and aroused kids has gotten through. We know now that we must get rid of the things we do not need in order to save the things we do need.

For example: water. From the moon, the earth is a deep blue, marbled with swirling clouds. Three fourths of our world is water. Almost all the water, though, is too salty or brackish to drink—97 percent. And most of the remaining 3 percent is too hard to get—it's frozen stiff in ice caps and glaciers. Where, then, can we get a glass of water to drink? From the 0.6 percent that is left—in lakes, streams, and reservoirs. And over half of that is underground! (So is sewage, poisonous chemicals, radioactive isotopes, and just about anything else we can dump down there.)

As long as the garbage and trash are collected regularly from the doorstep, few persons care at all where their refuse goes. Most still believe that all garbage is fed to hogs and the trash is hauled out to sea and dumped. Many believe that all states—rather than just a few—have passed pollution control laws that prevent industries from dumping dangerous wastes into rivers. The sad truth is that the man burning leaves in his own backyard may be fined, while a nearby steel mill is protected by some inequity of law.

How we really do get rid of wastes is sometimes shocking, sometimes frightening, and, many times, hopeful.

The heroes of this story are the ones who make it hopeful. They are the scientists and technologists who know that getting rid of waste is only a temporary measure. They are much like a boy whose mother says, "Get rid of those baseball cards!" or a girl who hears, "Aren't you a little old to have a drawer full of seashells?"

They ask first, "Do we really have to get rid of this?"

Wastes such as sewage or garbage or a rickety building can be a serious threat to safety. They must go. Others, such as unwanted automobiles, outdated airplanes or ships, are more of a housekeeping problem for the nation. Some waste, such as containers or paper, must be gotten rid of because more waste is already on the way to take its place.

But the scientists ask, "Could this item be used in some other way?"

The boy fits his baseball cards into a frame to hang in his room. The girl drills holes in her seashells and makes a necklace like no one else's. Perhaps, then, someone can find a use for piles of trash, a bunch of old newspapers, or even a leaky ship!

Researchers are constantly trying to find new uses for waste. Sometimes a new product appears, like that "useless" by-product of petroleum called gasoline. Qualified scientists are often helped in their search by grants of money from the Federal Government.

Some of the ideas for using waste sound odd and way out—just as did the first suggestion that man could fly or the first proposal that disease might be caused by impure drinking water rather than by the punishing anger of a Supreme Being. Some of the recommendations for getting rid of large amounts of waste may be inspired by genius. Some could turn out to be disastrous.

A law of physics that seems to be on the side of man, the maker and collector of things, says that nothing is ever *completely* gotten rid of. Try to burn it, still there are ashes and soot to dispose of. Try dumping it in the ocean, it floats back on the beaches. Try burying it, and it seeps into the drinking water, starts fires by spontaneous combustion, or forms shelters for rats.

We cannot afford to slow down research on the only real solution to getting rid of things—the eventual reuse of all wastes. Fortunately this puzzle attracts some of the most brilliant minds.

This book is the story of some of their efforts.

1

Fragmentizer and Carbecue

AUTOMOBILES

Getting rid of automobiles has been one of the most successful research projects in the past few years. But the solution took many complaining people, from congressmen down to town councilmen, to get the project started. And it took many technologists to get it on the road to success.

"We should drop them all into the ocean," said one congressman.

But the Department of Defense pointed out that a pile of steel automobile bodies would show up on sonar screens and foul up antisubmarine detection gear.

While the arguments rage over whether it would be better to build higher fences to hide the mess or to stuff all the old cars into abandoned coal mines, more than 6 million automobiles are discarded every year.

Often an angry car owner leaves his car right on the road where it stopped dead. When this happens, the city or state police must tow the car to an auto graveyard. Towing is expensive. When the last owner is located, a large bill is sent, as well as a stiff fine to remind

him that it is illegal to abandon an auto. In New York City, over 40,000 people get rid of their automobiles that way each year. At the auto graveyard, the abandoned car joins thousands of others waiting for their owners to either claim them or sign the legal papers that will turn them over to the junkman. It may be weeks before the junk dealer

A junkyard creeps into a creek near the nation's capital

FEDERAL WATER POLLUTION
CONTROL ADMINISTRATION

15

owns the car and can begin to untrim it, selling parts such as hubcaps, mirrors, and cushions.

At one time, stripped-down cars could be sold to steel mills as scrap metal for the furnaces. Suddenly, one day not too long ago, the junk dealers were told they could keep their autos. Steel mills all over the country were buying a new type of furnace. It was to be much more efficient. It also was much more particular about the amount and type of scrap metal it would accept. All those extras that were meant to make automobiles so much nicer were making the scrap metal very much worse. There was too much chromium and plastic. With the manufacturers designing lights here and there throughout the cars, there was too much copper wiring. The junk dealers watched their mountains of "money" turning into rust.

"The world's greatest untapped iron mines," shouted one lawmaker, "are those automobile junkyards!"

Not only did the metal piles represent a serious waste, but they looked so hideous. Everyone from the wife of the President of the United States to the junkman's neighbor complained. Old bathtubs, refrigerators, washing machines, and bedsprings added some variety as the heaps continued to grow.

Finally Congress passed a law about the junkyards that they had some control over—those facing a federal highway. The owners of those yards had the choice of cleaning up completely, beautifying, or hiding the mess from an irate public. If the owners refused, the state they were in would receive no more federal money for building highways. This law made the states pass more laws to enforce the rules. Flowers, fences, and billboards covered up some,

The world's greatest untapped iron mines
AMERICAN HOIST & DERRICK CO.

Location: Every city, U.S.A.
OGDEN CORP.

but in no time the autos had piled up behind them like a growing volcano.

At the beginning, automobiles were treated with much loving care. Barnum and Bailey proudly displayed one as the showpiece of their 1896 circus. By the 1930's, teen-agers could buy a "flivver," or "tin lizzy," for $25, with its paint as shiny as the day it left the factory. Gasoline cost anywhere from a nickel to 15 cents a gallon. Replacing a smashed fender cost only a few dollars. In those days, accidents between

Pancaked cars are loaded onto a flatbed trailer

A kiln where nonmagnetic ore is roasted with auto scrap

two cars were more rare than accidents with a belligerent cow that was not about to share the road. When the Pennsylvania Turnpike opened thirty years ago, the top speed was set hesitantly at a reckless 50 mph. A family could buy a car and expect to use it the rest of their lives. The automobile looked as if it could last fifty years—

and some of them have. Today a car is allowed to wear the Antique Car license plate when it is only twenty-five years old!

One good result of World War II was that it cleaned up the junkyards completely. Every piece of metal in this country, as well as in others, was sent off "to win the war." Housewives flattened every tin can after it was opened, putting it aside for the special collections. Unnecessary metal objects of all shapes and sizes joined the war effort. At least for a while, the metal was being used.

Through it all, the junk dealer has had one true friend—the teen-age boy. The boy who builds his own car or is fixing up an old model someone gave him sees nothing but beauty: a gem of a carburetor he could never afford to buy new, a Cadillac side-view mirror, cams and manifolds, and maybe a sharp black leather bucket seat. He

17

A load leaves for the Carbasher

sees other things too—the twisted mass of wreckage that was a new car until someone drove too fast. He talks to the man whose job it is to hose down the bloody cars as soon as they are brought in. Junkyards can be educational in a way.

But the mountains of unused iron began to worry people. The U.S. Bureau of Mines handed its laboratories a stiff assignment: "Turn old, junked auto scrap into something useful—quick!" Design engineers hunched over their drawing boards. Other technologists tackled the problem of the valuable copper that was trapped inside the scrap metal where it was not wanted. Copper has always been scarce, and it somehow had to be saved from whatever fate awaited the rest of the scrap.

Within months there were some startling discoveries.

The Bureau of Mines found that by adding the auto scrap to a low-grade nonmagnetic ore, taconite, they could actually come up with a better ore,

For a few minutes, the Carbasher grinds and scrunches

Result: a real "compact" car

18

artificial magnetite, which would be magnetic.

Technologists found they could leach out the valuable copper from the scrap. Selecting those pieces that contained copper, they could throw them into a vat, controlling the temperatures. The material that exited from the vat was rich in copper, and the scrap metal left behind was more valuable to the steel mills that had previously rejected scrap metal with copper in it. Because of the efforts of technologists, 80 percent of all the copper ever mined in this country is still in use.

Other inventive minds tried reducing scrap metal to iron powder. This, they found, could be rolled out into a foil or be formed into intricate shapes.

But the question of getting rid of all those rusty old cars seemed no closer to a solution. Even if a junk dealer could sell his autos as scrap metal, it would cost him a fortune to deliver them to the steel mill. A flatbed trailer could carry only six or eight cars at a time. If only they took up a little less space! All over the world, engineers were trying to think small.

Then inventions began to appear. They sounded crazy at first—but they worked! In the opinion of one junk dealer, "Not even a woman driver could change a car so thoroughly!"

In one minute the portable car flattener will level two cars down to a foot high. The car engine, made of cast iron, which lowers the value of the scrap metal, is removed first and melted down separately. Now a flatbed trailer

The Guillotine slices compacted cars into smaller pieces

AMERICAN HOIST & DERRICK CO.

can carry thirty of the squashed-down cars. Some junk dealers combine the flattener with the guillotine, or Iron Shark. A squeeze-box forces the flattened car into the guillotine-like shears, which slice it up as neatly as a loaf of bread.

Then there is the Carbasher. It is also portable, which means several junk dealers can put their money together and buy one Carbasher to move from one junkyard to another. It will bash 100 cars a day into pancakes that will stack up twenty or more on a trailer truck.

Another giant machine, the Fragmentizer, takes a car in its huge claw,

19

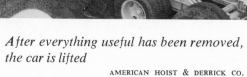

After everything useful has been removed, the car is lifted

AMERICAN HOIST & DERRICK CO.

A crane grabs the car from the lift and drops it into the Carbasher

AMERICAN HOIST & DERRICK CO.

In a few minutes it will be mashed flat

AMERICAN HOIST & DERRICK CO.

The Carbasher can compact 100 cars a day

AMERICAN HOIST & DERRICK CO.

20

shaking it up and down like an angry dog with a sock. Glass and small pieces of metal clatter into a pile below as the car is dropped, lifted, dropped again. Finally it is tossed like a broken toy onto another pile. A crane lifts the car from this pile and sets it on a ramp, to move uphill slowly on its last ride. Suddenly the car plunges down into a hammer mill that scrunches it as easily as the butcher's grinder turns meat into hamburger. By now the paint has been burned off and the twisted pieces of metal are about the size of a man's hand. At the base of the shaft, pieces that have copper in them are separated to go to a leaching plant so that the copper can be saved and used again. The remaining pieces are spewed onto a new pile. An electromagnet dips into this pile, attracting only the iron and steel, leaving behind mostly nonmetals like wood and plastic. The metallic pieces go into a final pile to await shipment to the steel mill. They are almost 98 percent pure steel.

The baling press turns autos into washing-machine size

AMERICAN HOIST & DERRICK CO.

Flattened car is loaded onto the hopper
AMERICAN HOIST & DERRICK CO.

An auto "log" is forced out through the shears

AMERICAN HOIST & DERRICK CO.

The Prolerizer, another type of fragmentizer, drops an auto down into the mouth of a shredder. In fifteen seconds the car has been shredded to pieces, free of dirt and paint. The Prolerizer has two hoppers. Out of one pours almost pure scrap metal for the steel mills. Out of the other comes junk metal, which can be used in other ways.

The Poor Man's Shredder, built by the makers of the Prolerizer for smaller cities that turn pale at the Prolerizer price tag, takes three minutes. It has two heavy, 8-foot-wide, crawler-type tractor treads mounted one above the other. Heavy spikes project from them. Moving at different speeds in the same direction, the spikes grind the car up between them.

The Big Squeeze Baler gained fame in the movie *Goldfinger,* where it played a major role by getting rid of the bad guy's car. A main compression ram crunches the car forward. Another jams it sideways. And three minutes after the ON button is pushed, the car is the size of a television set.

The Japanese have even less space for junkyards on their islands, so they invented the Carbecue. A car turns slowly on a spit—in a furnace so hot that the car is roasted faster than a hot dog. The lead melts at one temperature in the first oven and drips onto a con-

Scrap is chopped neatly for the steel mill
AMERICAN HOIST & DERRICK CO.

Autos—minus engines—take a last ride into the Fragmentizer

They come out the other end in pellet-size bits

veyor belt to be reused. The next oven is just hot enough to melt the aluminum. A third oven melts the valuable copper at a higher temperature. What is left of the car is squeezed by a hydraulic press into a small bale of almost pure metal scrap.

There is still something left over—even after these machines have done their jobs. The Bureau of Mines found a use for the leftover junk-metal scrap that is not good enough for steel mills. It is mixed with concrete in chunks about the size of a large suitcase. The cement-plus-iron blocks make strong building foundations, bridge supports, and retaining walls.

These "iron mines" may be solving their problems for today. But just around the corner lurks the next problem. Already many sports cars are built of fiber glass, with only the frames of metal. A chemical company has built a completely plastic car, which it expects to revolutionize the auto industry. This year's cars have 80 pounds of plastic in them. Tomorrow's junkyards may not look rusty, but so far no one seems to have thought about how to get rid of plastic cars.

2

Spare parts stock

PLANES AND TRAINS

THERE WAS no problem in getting rid of the earliest airplanes. The problem was to keep one together long enough to learn how to fly it and improve on it.

One cold day in December, 1903, the Wright brothers struggled with a flimsy crate of wood, wires, and cloth. They fastened it to the rigging that was to launch one of them into space. The flight of 120 feet was none too impressive and witnesses to the arrival of the Air Age were concerned more about getting close to a warm fire than about the flight. The next day, only a few newspapers mentioned the occasion.

Three more trials were flown that day before a gust of wind finally trounced the fragile craft seriously enough to end further tests. By the time Wilbur and Orville were warming themselves after lunch, their first airplane was already obsolete.

In the next seven years, other inventors improved so much on the Wright design that airplanes became four times as powerful and almost double in weight. One peculiarity of aircraft has

endured in the midst of progress: long before planes are worn out, they are outdated.

The airplane came out of infancy during World War I. Laughs turned to respect when lighter materials made planes more maneuverable. Larger gas tanks gave them greater range. But most important, in a few years airplane speed more than doubled. A single flier could drop a basket of bombs over a city and do more damage than a thousand soldiers.

Yet when peacetime came, most people felt the airplane had gone as far as it could go. A few conceded it might be useful for carrying mail. And air races were growing into an exciting sport. Still, airplanes would never be popular enough to manufacture in any quantity. It began to look as if airplanes would be gotten rid of before they even had a chance to get started.

But one general, William "Billy" Mitchell, insisted that airplanes should be developed further and not allowed to fade away. Even his friends thought he was being ridiculous when he said airplanes were our most important defensive weapon.

"Why, a single plane could sink a battleship!" he declared.

There was a chorus of outraged shouts from Navy men. Didn't he know that battleships were practically indestructible?

"They are as outdated as knights in armor," Mitchell retorted.

The Navy gave him a chance to prove it one day in 1921. A few old battleships and smaller ships were to be scuttled, and the Navy was willing to let Mitchell try with his airplanes. Some of the ships were damaged severely enough to sink. The rest were sunk immediately by direct hits. Airplanes had proven their usefulness. There was no more talk of getting rid of them.

Yet for the next few years, anyone could buy an old war plane for a few hundred dollars—with a couple of free flying lessons thrown in. No learner's permit or even a license was required. The plane engine's stalling point was only a few mph less than the plane's top speed. Weather reports were almost nonexistent. If it looked stormy, the pilot hunted a field before dark and prayed he had not chosen a newly plowed one. The planes had no landing lights, and what few fields there were had no lights either. Flying was a daytime sport.

Thrill-happy pilots were not easily frightened, though. They flew under bridges, raced beside trains, waving to the startled passengers, walked on the wings while flying over county fair crowds. An airmail pilot's life expectancy was judged by his insurance company—which would not sell him any life insurance—to be about eighteen months at best. Fortunately, during these growing-up years, airplanes carried only a few people. Some impatient businessmen paid to sit on the mailbags or on the floor just to get where they were going in a hurry. It came as a surprise to others that airplanes might be used for something besides sport and the mails. With the arrival of commercial airliners came the safety features that airplanes needed in order to stay around a while.

After World War II the country had an unusual surplus of planes. Many were sold to a scrapper to be melted down. A few more were adopted by cities. One city bought an unfinished B-29 Superfortress, named for the city, that had become outdated before it had even been completed. Another built an aviation memorial park around the five thousandth B-17 that had been built there. But there were still thousands of unwanted planes left to rot away. And where could thousands of airplanes be stored?

The answer rose suddenly, like a ghost, from the sands of the African desert. A B-24 bomber, the *Lady Be Good,* was uncovered by the stinging winds of a desert sandstorm. The plane sat there intact, where it had been forced down by enemy action sixteen years earlier. Air Force personnel inspecting her could hardly believe their eyes. The radios worked. The pumps still operated. There was even usable fuel left in the gas tanks!

Not only did the U.S. have too many airplanes; it also had deserts—with air dry as the air that preserved the *Lady Be Good*. Operation "Cabbage Patch" began with the moving of all the old planes loafing in airfields across the country to a 3,000-acre site in the desert near Tucson, Arizona. There helicopters, fighters, cargo planes, even outdated missiles, are parked in neat mile-long lines.

Part of 3,000 acres of planes waiting to be wanted

A decision must be made about each plane as it arrives—whether it should be repaired and put back in flying shape, or be stored and used as a source of parts, or be sold as scrap metal.

Over half the planes arriving at the storage center can be put back into use. The Government may use them for re-search, transport, or reconnaissance. Several cargo planes were recently used by the U.S. Department of Agriculture in active combat—against a fly that had caused a serious cattle disease. Two KC-97's were used in a secret experiment involving an orbiting space station. Some planes are sold to foreign countries that have no means for building their own planes.

The uses of airplanes are so varied and numerous that no nation can afford just to throw one away. Old planes are used for fire fighting, patrolling oil pipelines and power lines, surveying, fishing, newspaper work, church work, medical services, making aerial photos, advertising in the sky, exploring, and making maps and charts. Archaeologists use planes to spot ruins or to note unusual changes in the color of soil or vegetation that may conceal buried cities, ancient roads or paths, or fault lines caused by earthquakes. An airplane neatly rebuilt on the roof of a small restaurant in Pennsylvania looks as if it had just landed there. Some playgrounds provide a real head start for future pilots with a genuine airplane for the kids to climb through.

If the plane is to be stored, guns and special equipment are removed. New tires are replaced by old, useless ones. The fuel tanks are emptied. The inside is protected by fogcoating, and every crack is sealed with tape. Vital spots on the outside are protected from the weather by a covering of "Spraylat," a paintlike material that resists moisture and prevents rust from forming.

The dry Arizona desert takes care of the rest.

If the plane is a type that is still in use, the stored model can be a gold mine of parts. "Save lists" detail the parts most needed, and these are removed from the planes to be stored in a large warehouse. Sometimes an urgent call comes: "Ship a nose cone," or "Send us the tail section of a B-47 Boeing Stratojet!" One C-124 Globemaster, used as a test-bed for jet engines, has donated parts amounting to as much money as the plane cost new. This is because the parts cost so much more today than when the plane was built. These parts, even though they have been used, are worth infinitely more than some design that is still on the drawing boards.

This Stratojet tail section will be used to repair a damaged plane

USAF, MASDC

Stored aircraft are sprayed for protection from the weather

USAF, MASDC

If the plane is to be sold as scrap metal, it will first be stripped of every useful part. Then it is sold to the highest bidder. But the plane can leave the military yard in only one way—as an aluminum ingot. Cut into pieces and fed into a gas furnace to be melted down, it may become an automobile grill, a piston, an engine block, or even a frying pan.

Unused airplane parts are melted down

USAF, MASDC

Getting rid of the earliest trains was no problem either. Even though, unlike airplanes, trains did not have gravity working so hard against them, they did seem to have their own built-in self-destructors.

The invention of a steam engine that could be put on wheels and be made to pull a heavy load came shortly before the middle of the nineteenth century—a time when the U.S. especially needed help in delivering settlers and materials toward its western boundaries. The nation was ready, but the railroads were not.

The boilers in the steam engines exploded easily and often. But each time they did, improvements were made and locomotives got larger and heavier. The iron tracks, used until the first steel tracks were laid in 1867, often cracked under the weight of the locomotives, scattering the wooden train cars like toys. The U-shaped strap rail, in use until the T rail replaced it universally, had a tendency, when the train went too fast, to curl up and pierce the floors of the cars. One experimental locomotive in England earned itself the name of "Mac's Mangle" by its peculiar ability to get rid of station platforms.

Early signaling devices got rid of a few trains too. When the locomotive passed over a treadle, the weight changed the "clear" signal to a "danger" signal—sometimes. The treadle worked least when the traffic was heaviest. The invention of the telegraph was hailed as a great safety measure for trains, but it depended on human beings for its accuracy. Train traffic went in both directions over miles of single track. Small station huts were placed along the way, each with a stationmaster whose job was to receive and send the necessary wireless messages in Morse code. He might be instructed to hold a train on a small siding or else allow it to pass through. The stationmaster's job was lonely and he had to catch his sleep in between trains. Sometimes his dreams got confused with reality and the train that should have been stopped chugged on past, bound for a head-on collision.

Early brakes were a disgrace. When a crash appeared imminent, the brakemen ran from car to car, pulling on the brakes over each set of wheels by hand.

One train that will not escape the scrap heap

If the wreck did not finish the train, explosions from its gaslights often did.

Railroading in the United States really got going when the steel rail was laid—about a hundred years ago. At first, railroad cars as well as locomotives were outmoded almost as fast as they were built. The main thought in the mind of the passenger car builder was "getting there." But the United States is extremely large and the long trips made passengers demand comfort, even before speed. Many cars ended up back at the smeltery. But trains are made of heavy melting steel—this means they are too heavy to be broken, or fragmentized, as easily as an auto. They are sent to scrap reclamation yards. The more tenderhearted railroad men say the cars and engines are "retired." There the usable parts are salvaged—the trucks taken off, axles removed, wheels and springs saved. What is left must be pulled apart by overhead cranes and be cut by torch.

But trains, and particularly locomotives, have exceptionally loyal friends. Many railroad cars escape the scrap heap because admirers refuse to let them be junked. Sometimes they are sold to private buyers for vacation homes. Cabooses make comfortable small cottages. Circuses often buy outdated cars, remodeling them to suit their own particular needs. Since circuses travel at night, arriving early in the morning to set up their shows, pullman cars with their comfortable sleeping berths are important to the performers and circus hands.

Most city museums boast at least one engine—mainly because some railroad enthusiast wants children to know how it feels to be small and look up at a huge puffing engine. Getting a monster inside the museum is no small feat either! When Philadelphia's Franklin Institute decided to put a real moving engine inside where children could climb on it to play engineer, the museum wall had to be chopped out. And since the nearest railroad station was several blocks away, two sets of movable rails were laid for the engine to roll down the street. As soon as the locomotive was pulled onto one set of rails, a tired old horse would lug the other set of rails from behind to set them in front so the engine could be pulled toward its destination. It was three days before the engine reached the museum's temporary door and rolled inside. Since that day, thousands of children have clambered up its ladders.

Old #60000 rides down the street on movable rails

THE FRANKLIN INSTITUTE,
PHILADELPHIA, PA.

At the Franklin Institute, the engine is pushed and pulled through its special "doorway"

THE FRANKLIN INSTITUTE,
PHILADELPHIA, PA.

Many old steam trains are still chugging down backcountry railroad tracks, taking railroad fans on excursions. For a few miles, passengers can imagine the good old days when smoke and cinders poured in the windows and the whistle's sound echoed in the valleys. Those same whistles, donated by railroad companies, still announce quitting time in many local factories. Locomotive bells have been given to churches and schools.

As freight trains have gained in importance—because they bring in the most money—many passenger cars have gone out of date. Restaurants called diners had their beginnings as real dining or parlor cars pushed off the tracks by more glamorous cars designed to make railroad travel more attractive. Diners began small, but their popularity forced them to grow and add rooms. Today it is rare to see a diner that looks anything like a real dining car at all. One man bought three beautiful old train cars, set them on real tracks, and turned them into a popular restaurant. The "passengers" eat in the plush lower berths or in the velvet-decorated dining car that was

Going to dinner in a real diner

COACH INN, FORT WASHINGTON, PA.

30

*Once the private car of a millionaire—
now a restaurant*

once a millionaire's private domain. Customers have all the sensation of eating in a dining car, except for the sway that used to pitch water from the glasses when the train rattled around a fast curve!

Trains combine size and mobility in such a way that they have been used as hospitals and schools, especially in areas inaccessible to cars or trucks.

They carry museums, traveling exhibits, and libraries to small towns or to large remote areas like Alaska.

The future poses bigger and bigger problems in the disposal of trains and planes.

There is talk of building trains that will be more powerful and faster, but the problem of getting rid of them will always be the same. No matter how old a railroad car may be or how wheezy an ancient locomotive is, it will still have its champions who would rather eat in, live in, ride in, or go to school in a train than anything else in the world.

But airplanes seem to get larger and harder to dispose of all the time. The new jumbo jets carry more than twice the passengers of the largest standard jets, have wide movie screens and even a penthouse lounge room. The Wright brothers could have made their entire 120-foot flight inside the cargo space of Lockheed's new plane, the *Moby Jet*!

When a jumbo jet becomes obsolete, disposal will be a real headache.

3

New life for old hulks

SHIPS

Sʜɪᴘs have been around for thousands of years. But it was not until 1888 that anyone really wanted very much to get rid of one.

Sailing probably began on the Nile River. There, the prevailing wind puffed out the cotton sails and blew the Egyptians up the river. What might have been a very fast ride was slowed down by the current, which was always going in the other direction. When the sailors were ready to come home, they lowered the sails and drifted lazily back.

Sometime around 300 B.C., man discovered he was no longer limited to going with the wind or current. He learned to tack with his sails. This art of zigzagging was taken up enthusiastically by the Phoenicians, who appreciated getting places faster, and soon their ships were seen everywhere. Sailboats grew larger and their sails grew more complicated. More sails meant more men to handle them, and that in turn meant larger ships. Many square-riggers lumbered clumsily into storms and failed to come out of them.

No problem getting rid of those ships!

By the time gold was discovered in California, there was a rush at the ticket offices of sleek clipper ships. The gold seeker from the East who managed to book passage on a clipper ship around Cape Horn had a mental picture of himself riding in a gently swinging hammock toward the Golden West while his less fortunate forty-niners slogged across the muddy continent. He learned his mistake soon after embarkation, when it became apparent that storage space had been given to passengers instead of to food. The captain had reasoned they would probably all be too seasick to eat anyway. But as soon as the ship arrived in San Francisco harbor, the seasickness disappeared magically and the passengers disappeared into the hills after the precious metal. The hard part was—the crew disappeared too! At one time the Bay was so full of deserted ships that a man could walk almost across it without getting wet. Ships began to rot at their moorings. No crews could be found—even among the unsuccessful gold seekers—to sail home again. Many a ship owner quit too and made his own pile of gold by beaching his ship and opening a hotel at sky's-the-limit prices. Some of the less lucky ships became foundations for the first San Francisco waterfront docks.

About this time, a British ship designer named Brunel built a new kind of ship. To the great surprise of everyone, it did not sink. He built another ship like it but five times as large as any ship afloat. It was made of iron and was christened the *Great Eastern*. The *Great Eastern* began a new era in shipbuilding in 1858, but people watching the launching never realized that a new era in shipscrapping had also arrived.

This huge ship was designed to end seasickness for all time, since it was longer than the trough of the biggest storm wave ever measured. Unfortunately, the ship was to run into larger storms. She carried five funnels for steam, and she also carried six masts for sails. She could have carried 4,000 passengers too, but there were never more than a hundred who wanted to sail on her.

The *Great Eastern* was plagued with trouble—from the day a workman was killed and fell between her double hulls, where his body could not be found, until the day the ship's owners decided to get rid of her. In 1888, she was sold to a ship-breaker whose luck ran out the day he bought her. In August, a crew started towing her to Liverpool to be broken up, but a sudden storm caused the ship to roll so violently that the cable broke. Risking their lives, the crew rode out the storm, keeping as near the lurching giant as they dared. When the weather finally calmed down, it was several days before they managed to tow her into port. All winter they auctioned off pieces of the ship and her equipment. Then in May the scrapping began. But the iron hulls resisted every blow of the hammers designed to break up lesser ships. No torch had been invented yet, nor had any other device for taking apart an iron ship. The builders had never even thought of taking it apart.

The only way to separate the steel plates was to pound the rivets loose. Day after day the pounding had little effect. After weeks had gone by with only a few rivets loosened, someone decided to fight iron with iron, and the wrecker's ball was invented. The huge iron ball clanged incessantly against the steel, day and night. For ten miles away, people suffered and named it the "headache ball." Gradually, one by one, the plates were worked loose. The body of the workman and that of a missing boy helper were found, and the shipbreakers began to feel the curse was finished. After eighteen months of ceaseless pounding, the scrappers finally reached the keel.

Today shipwreckers use the oxyacetylene torch. First the machinery is removed and sold. Electrical motors, hoists, derricks, wiring, air conditioning, and navigational instruments are sold at home or abroad. Often the whole ship, unless it was a Government

33

ship, is sold to another country that will pay higher prices just to get the steel. They can sail or tow it home to be taken apart in their own country where labor is cheaper. A U.S. Government ship, however, must be dismantled in a U.S. shipyard, although anyone may buy the steel after the ship is taken apart. Sometimes the steel plates are sold separately to build steel barges.

Some years, old ships were bought by the Navy for target practice. Others were bought and loaded with obsolete ammunition and equipment. The ammunition was no longer wanted in this country, but it might do a great deal of damage if the wrong people got hold of it, so the ships and their loads were sunk in the ocean—a good example of double getting-rid-of-it!

Old ships are often sunk to form breakwaters. Hatch covers and openings are welded shut, except for the few that are opened to allow water to pour in and sink the ship. All the ingredients for cement—dredged materials, sand, gravel, boulders, and limestone—are pumped into the sunken hull. Result? An instant pier, dock, or breakwater.

Often only part of a ship is scrapped. The bow or stern, or even the mid-body, can be used to repair another ship, or to build a whole new ship. The Japanese developed the first 3-D enlargement of a ship, which was conducted in much the same way that they create their wooden-block puzzles. The body of the ship was divided across in three parts: bow, stern, and mid-body.

Blasting a tanker mid-body neatly in two

NEWPORT NEWS SHIPBUILDING PHOTO

A retired ship becomes a floating college dormitory

STEVENS INSTITUTE OF TECHNOLOGY

Then two new parts were constructed between those parts, making the entire ship longer. Next the upper deck was raised to make the ship higher. Then, slicing the ship down the center lengthwise, workers added a new section to make the ship wider. The size of the ship was almost doubled! The name of the ship was changed, because it is the custom in shipyards when a ship is reconverted in any way to change the name—to prove it is a really "new" ship.

The *Queen Elizabeth I* was not old or damaged. She was not even tired when her owners decided she was outdated. Not many people have the time nowadays for leisurely ocean voyages, even on a ship with restaurants, libraries, swimming pools, clubrooms, a movie theater, and rooms for 2,300

A new jetty—built of tanker sections

NEWPORT NEWS SHIPBUILDING PHOTO

guests. Her smokestacks could have made garages for two freight engines. But no one wanted her taken apart. She may become a convention center in sunny Florida.

Just when teachers think their students have used every excuse imaginable for not studying, someone comes up with a new one—seasickness! A former luxury liner became a college, and its students sailed around the world while studying. Another ship, honorably discharged after war service and serving time as a luxury liner, found a career in college. She is a temporary college dormitory, docked on the Hudson River opposite New York City. The boys love her, even though at very low tide she may list a bit to one side. They put their history books under two legs of the pool table in the recreation room and keep right on playing.

The superships have already started to arrive. One tanker is the size of three football fields. Each of its eighteen storage tanks could hold a nine-story building. But the newest tankers will each be as long as the Empire State Building lying down. They will be too large to enter most harbors, so special docks must be built with facilities for pumping their loads into cities they cannot reach. Each ship will be large enough to hold all the oil pumped out of Kuwait in twenty-four hours! Their builders have not begun to worry about how to get rid of them. Perhaps they should remember the *Great Eastern*.

4

Dismantling artists

BUILDINGS

"BUT those buildings are *new!*"
An army of bulldozers, crawler loaders, and cranes scrunched down the flower-lined streets. Each building on their seek-and-destroy list was less than three years old. Was it an invasion?

It was the end of the 1964–65 New York World's Fair, and for the engineers and wreckers this was to be the best part! Rarely does a wrecker have a chance to lay his demolishing tools on something new and beautiful. There were exotic shapes—ovoid, clamshell, umbrella. How easily would they come down? Some were built of strange new materials. Would they crack, crumble, or even explode if the wrong bolt came out first?

As for the engineers, this might be the only chance they would ever have to test the strength of some of the unusual shapes and materials. Some buildings were loaded with pig iron and sandbags. Supports were stressed with hydraulic jacks. Then came the attackers—bulldozers, the skull cracker, and a new invention designed to vi-

brate a building violently. What was learned in that classroom will become history for architects and designers.

Written into the Fair lease was the agreement that each building would see to its own destruction so that the land could be cleared as soon as possible.

A crane batters down the inside walls

37

Some buildings were built with this in mind, having a basement area underneath into which the whole building could collapse. A few nudges by the bulldozer pushing a soil blanket over it, and the building was gone forever. Others had been sold and had to be taken apart with the greatest care so that they could be reconstructed somewhere else. On these, giant cranes started at the top and worked downward, following exactly the opposite order from their construction, laying the pieces gently on the ground. There they were marked in proper sequence for the builder who had to put the puzzle back together again at the new site.

For the buildings being demolished, it was over quickly. A pair of bulldozers shoving together in two vital spots could make a small building fold up like a house of cards. Others had to be smashed repeatedly with the skull cracker, a steel ball the size of a barrel suspended from a crane.

Tearing down buildings has been a challenge ever since the first man built himself a castle that his enemy could not get into. Soon whole towns enclosed themselves safely within walls. At first the enemy amused himself with hurling missiles over the top of the walls into the courtyards below. But that way he could not see what havoc he was wreaking. Besides, there was always the chance he would wreck something valuable that would be his —after the battle was over.

So attention focused on the main gate, and the battering ram was in-

Find the handsome Colonial market in this warehouse

Carefully peeling away the years

Demolition exposes the original beams and supports

A Colonial landmark in Philadelphia's Society Hill today

*Things looked bad for the Neave and Abercrombie houses
when the wrecker was called in*

vented. The ram required much auxiliary equipment. There must be archers to shoot down those guarding the gate approaches, shield holders to protect the batterers when boiling oil was pouring down from above, and replacements for the wounded batterers. The weapon itself was usually the toughest tree the men could lift, with one end bound in iron, shaped to look like a ram's head with horns. At least it looked that way until after it hit the wooden gates' iron hinges. A later battering ram was attached by chains to a wheeled support and could be swung at the gate even better and by fewer men.

Cannons were considered a great improvement in the technique of demolition—especially by the demolishers, who could now stand much farther away from the scene of action. At first they fired only rocks, then iron balls. Many old brick houses from American Revolutionary War days still hold cannonballs stuck halfway through their brick walls, probably having caused nothing more serious than broken dishes.

Wrecking a house as a peaceful occupation, however, involves more knowledge and much more patience than pulverizing one with a cannon. If building is an art, then certainly unbuilding is too. As a house is being constructed, it becomes stronger with each support that is added. But when it is being taken apart, it becomes weaker and weaker. In addition to having the building grow more shaky with each day's work, the wrecker has an added hazard. Since the buildings he tears down are usually old, their building plans often have been lost years before. He must guess, hoping he's right, at what he will find inside the walls. In the early days of the U.S., carpenters had handmade nails, which they used very sparingly, mainly to frame the doors and windows. Wood joists were cut and expertly shaped to fit tightly without nails. As homesteaders moved westward, timber was very plentiful, but carpenters were not. So they built their own "balloon frame" houses, named because of the light and flimsy construction. Balloon frames could be built without using heavy frame timbers by almost any handyman with a package of the new machine-made, cheaper nails. These are two types of construction the wrecker might run into. There is no school except Experience that can teach him how to tear down a building.

Buildings are usually torn down because they are out of date. Schools with open stairwells, for example, are condemned because experience has shown that a fire will fan upward quickly if such a draft is provided. Doors closing off the stairway are required now. Sometimes whole blocks of buildings are leveled to make room for a new bridge entrance or turnpike. In a larger city, an owner may have a building torn down because he can collect twice as much money by turning his property into a parking lot.

Before wrecking begins, a wooden canopy is constructed over the sidewalk. Sometimes the street is closed off to protect people from being hurt by falling objects—also to protect the wrecker from "sidewalk experts" who ask questions and give advice freely.

Chutes carry the smaller pieces directly into a truck, while a hoist lowers the larger pieces. Jackhammers, with a hundred punches a minute, and stopers, which deliver twice as many per minute, are much like the old battering rams. A crawler loader has a "stinger" on the end which plunges through a cement wall just the way the doctor's hypodermic needle hits the target. Small bulldozers are used high up in large buildings to shove off debris.

"We sell everything but the dust," says one famous wrecker.

Saving the pieces and selling them was a new idea in 1900. Until then, a building was wrecked because it had no use. Today's wrecker makes most of his money by reselling parts of what he is getting rid of. Sentiment often plays a large part. When a favorite old New York hotel was condemned, buyers paid three times the original

The walls are made to collapse inward
CLEVELAND WRECKING CO.

price for an old lamp or chair that once stood in its lobby. Thrilled shoppers buy doorknobs and faucets from a millionaire's mansion. The Brooklyn Museum has a sculpture garden of figures that used to look down on the New York crowd from a skyscraper. One wrecker is still sensitive about the time he took three oil paintings from a Midwest hotel and sold them to a friend for $1 each. By that afternoon the friend had already sold the first painting for $350!

In spite of precautions, accidents do happen. Workers must wear helmets, thick-soled shoes, and clothing with no pockets or openings. One worker was tossing long boards out of a third-floor window when a nail caught on his trousers. Before he could stop himself, he was whisked out of the window after the planks. Fortunately he landed in a pile of laths—small wood—with only minor bruises.

The demolition ball cannot be used in any building that is attached to another because of the reverberations. One day after California had had several frightening earthquakes, a wrecker dropped the skull cracker on the cement floor of a vacant hotel. For half a mile, people panicked with rumors of new earthquakes. Explosives, which would so often make his job easier, are used sparingly by the wrecker. For one thing, he is afraid of the damages people will claim. "If I used dynamite," said one wrecker, "everyone living within hearing distance who had a broken window would blame me for

it." When blasting is used, the explosive charges are attached to the structural columns. When they are detonated, the building collapses within itself instead of all over the street. By removing certain columns, wreckers can sometimes prepare the building in such a way that it will be top-heavy and fall just where they want it to.

Some of the newer methods of building have led to challenges for the wrecker. For example, posttension concrete-beam construction is cabled, holding the parts in tension. If these cables were broken out of sequence, the concrete beam could explode. Campers know that a tent will stay up even if only a few of the ropes are attached to pegs in the ground. They also know that if a certain few ropes are cut, their tent will collapse flat. Some new buildings arrive at the building site all ready to be bolted together like plastic model stations for toy train platforms. This is called the tilt-up method of building. But the "tilt-down" method requires that tearing down such buildings be exactly in reverse. Removing even the smallest wrong bolt could cause a collapse.

Another hazard is the danger of taking down the wrong building. It makes a good joke—because it does happen! Two old houses on opposite corners of a street were sold to rival gasoline companies. But Company A was able to set up an appointment with the wrecker before Company B. The wrecker's man visited the spot and telephoned the office to say the one to be wrecked was on the southeast corner. Next morning, just as the first wall of the house on the southeast corner collapsed, a car drove up and a man asked what was going on. There are not too many answers a wrecker can think of at such a moment. He had torn down Company B's building! Of course, Company B was delighted, because it could now have a two-week head start on the other gas station.

Once in a long while, treasures are found. They range from archaeological treasures to thousands of dollars in Confederate money. But not too much data is available on exactly what treasures are found in the form of useful money or jewels. This is because of a "finders keepers" rule that is a sort of tradition. It says that any workman opening up a wall and finding a treasure gets to keep it. He doesn't usually say, "Hey, look what I found!" He just leaves quietly.

5

Historian's delight

CONTAINERS

MAN MAY HAVE BEEN born a collector. But what he was going to collect things in was left for him to figure out.

Nature supplied a few hints. The bottle-gourd tree provided good jars and bowls. The hard shells of pomegranates—a mouth-puckering fruit—made cups. Birch bark curled up easily and suggested small containers and boxes. Bamboo made scoops. And green bamboo is still used by some tribes for cooking utensils. Natives of the Kalahari Desert region still bury emergency water supplies in ostrich-egg containers. These earliest containers must have been very easy to get rid of, because archaeologists complain that they are almost impossible to find.

While man was hunting and warring, the fewer possessions he had, the faster he could run. But when he settled down and began to think of having a home, the need for something better in the way of containers arose. No one knows which he invented first—baskets or pottery. Some basket makers had no pottery, although they smeared clay on the outside of their baskets to make them hold water. Some pottery makers had no baskets.

Baskets and pottery may look flimsy and breakable, but they have shown a remarkable ability to stay around. Baskets dating back to 5000 B.C. have been found. Sometimes a few bits of grain or even a body are still in them, giving an idea as to their use. Pottery may be breakable, but once the pieces drop on the ground, the potsherds rarely break into smaller pieces and cannot decay. This is a feature much appreciated by archaeologists because they can often find and fit together most of the pieces of a shattered pot by concentrating their search in a small area.

Discarded pottery, whether broken or unbroken, provides scientists with the first history books—gifts of a people who probably could not write. Often pots were painted with scenes depicting war or peace, or the food or clothing of the people. Sometimes our earliest knowledge of inventions such as glassblowing or of technological

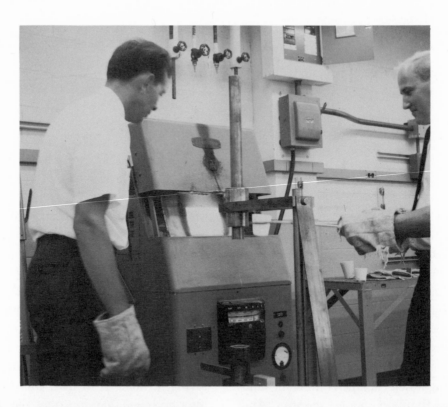

Going . . . going . . . gone! Dr. Samuel F. Hulbert, inventor of dissolving glass, and Dr. C. C. Fain photograph their successful experiment at Clemson University. Photos taken at two-hour intervals show a glass disk ½-inch thick melting into water

advances such as the domestication of animals has come from paintings on ancient pottery. Many scientists believe that the wheel began as a pottery-making tool and only later advanced to its valuable position as a means of transportation. Archaeologists can tell quickly whether the pottery of a certain people was made with or without the use of a potter's wheel.

When man tired of warring and began to settle and trade, he found that life among neighbors required more equipment. If he wanted a certain type of jar or longed for the sort of woven hammock his neighbor slept in, there was only one way to get it peacefully— by trading. But trading often meant long trips and carrying heavy loads. That would require larger containers. Primitive man made skin sacks for his wife's back, with a leather strap to go around her forehead to help balance the load. He made the first bottle to carry his water, using the stomach of some animal, plugging up the leaks at both ends. Sometimes he could persuade an ox to drag a slide car. The slide car had two shafts of wood that dragged along the ground with a box or basket held securely between them. Fortunately this carrier had to last only until the invention of the wheel.

Glass bottles were made in Egypt about 1500 B.C., but they were only for the noblemen until a smart craftsman discovered how to blow glass bottles. Blown glass became very popular about the first century B.C. The Venetians decided, in A.D. 1291, that they would become famous for making glass. But to accomplish their aim they had to make sure no one else could make glass cheaper. They kidnapped every glassblower they could catch and shipped them all to the island of Murano, near Venice. Guards patrolled the streets of Murano, constantly on the lookout for secret agents from other countries. The glassblowers were given every comfort and convenience. They were also warned that their breath would stop suddenly if they dared tell any of the secrets of glassblowing. The coup failed. The secret leaked out, and glass became a part of daily life.

Bottles were made to last—and they do. At first, milk bottles and soda bottles were returned to the factory to be refilled and used over. In most foreign countries, bottles are still carried to the store to be filled. But in this country, they began to pile up in the trash, along the roadsides, under the sand at the beach, in the rivers and lakes.

Finally the one-way tripper arrived. One-way bottles are made of such lightweight glass that they are weakened by the pressure of the gas in a carbonated drink. Even if the bottles do not break, they cannot be used for sodas again. So the piles of bottles get higher. Added to them are the one-way TV dinner trays, one-way plastic milk bottles, and one-way aluminum soda cans.

A professor in California has been watering aluminum cans and plastic jars in his "garden" now for six years and reports not the slightest sign of deterioration. These containers, buried in landfill, will probably look the same to the archaeologist in the twenty-fifth century as they look today. Burning is the only solution for getting rid of them. Yet there are many reasons why they should not be burned: the burning of plastics releases poisonous fumes into the already polluted air, and aerosol cans explode dangerously in intense heat. Broken glass and aluminum cans, if they were not mixed with the other trash, could be melted down and re-used. Tin cans could be melted down to save the copper in them.

If Rip Van Winkle woke up in the U.S. today, he would probably starve before he found anything to eat. There is a chance he could not even find a grocery store, because the outdoor fresh fruit and vegetable stand that always marked the neighborhood grocery is now considered unsanitary. Inside, everything is wrapped tightly in boxes, bags, plastic, Styrofoam, and shrink wrap. The butcher is usually nowhere to be seen, although his meats are in the case, prewrapped in packages too tough to break with the poke of a finger. No customers carry baskets on their arms. No smiling grocer stands ready with his long-handled gadget for lifting items down from the high shelves —there are rarely any high shelves. But Rip would get something he never got at home in the Catskills. Along with his week's supply of groceries, he would get 18 pounds of packaging!

Why is food packaged the way it is? Even though fruits and vegetables have been picked and are no longer growing, they must still have oxygen. Also, they still give off carbon dioxide and heat. But in order to keep them from spoiling fast, the grocer must slow down their loss of moisture.

The housewife used to choose her fresh carrots by the healthy appearance of their green tops. But the Department of Agriculture noted that the greenery was looking far fresher than the carrots did! After making tests, scientists found that the green tops were drawing all the moisture out of the carrots themselves, causing the part the housewife really wanted fresh to be shriveled and dried out. When plastic bags first appeared, they made even potatoes look gift-wrapped. But there were no holes in the bags and the effect on the potatoes was the same as the effect of a plastic mask on a Halloweener's face:

Junk that is too valuable to burn
AMERICAN PAPER INSTITUTE

47

things get hot! The heat captured inside the plastic bag made the potatoes rot twice as fast as normally, until someone thought to make holes in the bag. Meats and baked goods are packaged especially well to keep dirt from getting into them—an important point to consider now that they are displayed where even the smallest person can touch them.

Scientists all agree that packages are very necessary. They also agree that packages are a problem. But they do not agree on what to do about it.

There is the make-it-attractive group. These designers concentrate on making the package so interesting that the buyer cannot bring himself to part with it—thus keeping it out of the trash. Corrugated boxes are made with psychedelic designs, in mod colors and all sizes. They can be used as temporary furniture. Jars are fashioned in eye-catching shapes to be used as vases,

Attractive containers are even harder to get rid of

drinking glasses, candle holders. Children will not part with plastic cereal containers in the shape of teddy bears or jelly glasses with elephants on them.

Next there is the no-package-package group. They have ideas like spraying a protein coating, derived from corn, on foods to protect them against loss of vitamins and spoilage. The coating is perfectly safe to eat and is used now on dried fruits, nuts, enriched rice, and frozen dehydrated foods. Someday soon it may also be sprayed on cheese in place of the wax coating that must be removed before eating, or on fresh vegetables and fruits in place of miles of plastic wrap.

In the no-package-package group is a new type of glass that may be the answer to the 26 billion bottles thrown away every year. The glass is coated on the inside as well as the outside by a water-resistant film. When the bottle is smashed, the glass will dissolve in plain water, or hydralize. In three or four days, nothing remains but a little puddle.

Another no-package is the plastic bag used to hold laundry bleach or bluing. Tossed into the laundry, it dissolves before the washing is finished. But the prize will go to the scientist who can come up with a container that is as successful as the ice cream cone!

While the container waste problem is growing, so are the containers. Food is shipped to market centers now in much larger containers so that a forklift truck can do all the lifting. They are built tough enough to withstand both

Getting rid of these is only temporary
AMERICAN PAPER INSTITUTE, INC.

The baling machine makes neat bundles
AMERICAN PAPER INSTITUTE, INC.

The cartons will be weighed before storing
AMERICAN PAPER INSTITUTE, INC.

film, like that which covers four to five apples in the grocery, is now large enough and strong enough to wrap around pounds of books for shipping without cartons.

Large cartons from supermarkets, factories, and department stores are collected and returned to paper-stock plants. There they are unloaded, baled by machine, and stored until they are repulped and made into more cartons.

high vertical pressures created when they are stacked in trailer trucks or warehouses and sudden jolts such as abrupt stops at turnpike-travel speeds.

Every time an automobile is assembled, 400 pounds of refuse is left behind. Most of it consists of the containers used to ship the various parts to the assembly plant. King-size shrink

Soon they will be repulped—to become new cartons!
AMERICAN PAPER INSTITUTE, INC.

49

The largest containers are those used to ship long distances. At the warehouse the container, like a giant-size shoe box, is packed with merchandise and lifted onto a railroad flatcar or a trailer truck. At the dockside it takes just sixty seconds to lift a 25-ton container into the ship's hold. The customer in Tokyo or London receives merchandise that has not even had a chance to break or get lost since it left the factory. Someday when it's time to get rid of these, they will make nice summer cottages or fishing camps.

6

Products from refuse

WOOD

IN THE REGIONS of the Middle East, where written history began, getting rid of wood was unthinkable. Stealing a tree was a crime because the trees belonged to the wealthy landowners, who often had to pay taxes on them. One ancient Assyrian recorded for posterity that his tax collector had counted 49,300 trees on his property.

Wood was so precious in early Egypt that even the pharaoh's carpenter could not afford to throw away a board with a knothole in it. Instead, he carved out the knot carefully, inserting a plug of matching wood so deftly that the defect hardly shows thousands of years later. A carpenter in the treeless Middle East was no ordinary laborer. He was a skilled artisan.

By contrast, the tribes living in northern Europe had plenty of trees— at first. The northerners built homes of wood, filled them with heavy wood furniture, heated them with wood logs, and cooked their food on wood charcoal. The wood supply began dwindling at an alarming rate. When there came a choice between heating people's

houses with charcoal or building the king's navy of wooden ships, there really was no choice at all. By the tenth century, some regions had already forbidden the making of charcoal. The charcoal shortage did give a boost to the coal industry and soon cities were choking with sulfur fumes.

The wood shortage did not end until the day the colonists landed on the shores of the New World. There, the scarcity of wood back home had a peculiar effect on the settlers. Suddenly they saw more trees in one glance than they had seen in a lifetime. They could hardly wait to start chopping. Houses, factories, ships, docks, even roads, were built of trees.

The men who had financed the Virginia colony informed Captain John Smith soon after his arrival in the New World that they expected a steady flow homeward of gold and silver. The investors wanted to see some return on their investment. About $8,000 would do for a starter, they wrote, pointing out what the Spaniards had been bringing home from Mexico. Smith was wor-

Wood slabs waiting to be debarked and chipped. Each stack makes one mouthful for the lifter

AMERICAN FOREST INSTITUTE

ried. He knew that if the Jamestown colony was to receive another shilling, he must find something of value to send home. From the way the Indians had accepted his gifts of cheap glass beads, he was sure they had no gold or silver. But there were trees. Captain Smith put the colony to work chopping wood and manufacturing "naval stores," so called because they are necessary to the shipbuilding trades. Tar, pitch, ashes for soap, turpentine, and some timber —the first cargo of colonial manufactured goods saved the colony.

Trees were not on the list of early American worries. Few men were like William Penn, who had named Penn's Woods and wanted to see his land kept in woods. Penn ordered that an acre of forest be left standing for every five acres cut down. Oddly enough, no one ever seemed to think of replanting trees. John Chapman, better known as Johnny Appleseed, planted thousands in the 1800's—all apple trees.

Gifford Pinchot grew up loving the forests of Pennsylvania. When he decided to become a forester, there was not a single forestry school in the United States. But Europe, with centuries of valuable experience in making mistakes and learning to value trees, had excellent forestry education. In 1898, President Theodore Roosevelt appointed Pinchot his Chief Forester.

The new Chief Forester soon discovered that people had been doing much too good a job of getting rid of wood. He began by confronting the people with the shocking facts about their disappearing forests. It was the right place to start. People armed with the facts of a situation can wield tremendous power. Logging companies, long accustomed to using only one third of a tree and leaving the rest to be stumbled over in the woods, were the first to feel that power. Forestry schools began, and fire lookout stations were set up. Best of all, trees were planted. Most people had just assumed that trees re-seed themselves successfully. The Douglas fir, for example, does reseed, but the tiny firs will never grow where the seed drops. They must have full sun, and this means planting by hand.

With new tools, there is now less wood waste. A gas-powered saw guided

Sawdust and shavings are compacted into clean . . .

. . . logs for campfires and homes

by one man takes less than ten minutes to do what two men used to do in a half hour. In place of the dragging of long logs through forest trails, shortened logs are now carried by cable systems that look like ski tows. Diesel trucks haul the logs to the sawmill, where the "electric elephant" can unload 40 tons of timber in one bite. Jets of water under high pressure peel off the bark in a few minutes. Thinner saw-blades mean less sawdust waste. A new hydraulic shear can snip smaller trees, thinning the forest as easily as cutting dandelions. Helicopters are used to plant seeds or to help "top" trees. Foresters study new ways to cut logs to get the maximum use from each tree. Laser beams may help with future log-cutting.

The lumber industry still produces much waste, even with such concentration on not wasting wood. Researchers know how much is demanded of trees, and they begin their study of getting rid of waste by improving the trees themselves. Trees can be made to grow taller, thicker, or straighter. They can be made to grow faster—even fast enough to kill themselves. Genetics experts can now make trees more resistant to fires, insects, or diseases. Trees can be grown especially to provide lumber for building or pulp for paper. But still there is much waste.

Wood waste comes in the form of chips, sawdust, fibers, and shavings. In the old days, these were all tossed into a furnace and burned. Occasionally the heat from the burning was used to generate steam to run the lumbermill en-

Planing-mill shavings make good bedding for farm animals

gines. Many more of these pieces were dropped on the forest floor and left.

The old logger of 1880 would never believe what can be done with wood chips! A layer of wood chips pads the rough spots on a ski slope, particularly where the ground is very rough or rocky. After a good snow covers the slope, the ski lifts begin operating. Spread in a large circle around growing trees, wood chips discourage weeds and help the tree get all the water it needs. They insulate the soil around the newly planted trees, soaking up water and holding it like a sponge. Under fruit trees, chips make a good cushion for the fruit to drop on. Mixed with vegetable or animal wastes, wood chips make a good, safe fertilizer. In animal cages or livestock pens, they make good bedding. Chips are used on the divider strip of some turnpikes, particularly where caring for growing

grass would be a problem and where gravel produces too much glare for night driving. Sometimes chips are used in landscaping, where they prevent soil erosion. Wood chips are used to make paper, and chips from the longleaf pine are turned into turpentine, resin, and pine oil.

A bulldozer atop a sawdust mountain

The sawdust the old logger had such a time getting rid of now has many uses too. Ever since a man first twirled two sticks together to make a fire, sawdust has been a good kindling. Campers like the clean long-burning logs they can buy at any grocery—made of pressed sawdust. Sawdust is used for packing delicate objects or as an insulation in packing foods. It helps the school janitor sweep the floor by giving the flyaway dust something to cling to. Ground up and mixed with glue, chalk, clay, or linseed oil, sawdust can be formed into attractive, permanent, ornamental ceilings. Some diet foods even use sawdust, since it swells up, filling the stomach, when water is added. Sawdust sprinkled on spilled oil makes the oil easier to clean up. But when oil has spilled in the sea, sawdust clings to the oil and makes it sink. The

Wood fibers, which used to be thrown away, can be molded like plastic

Bark of the redwood tree is used to package fresh fruit

mess may be out of sight, but when the next storm comes and stirs the ocean floor, the problem returns. In Sweden, powdered pine tree bark spilled accidentally onto a pond of oily water. Surprisingly, it formed into large cakes that did not sink and could easily be cleaned from the pond. The bark is now sold for cleaning oil messes, but it is too expensive for use in some of the large oil slicks plaguing the shores and beaches.

Silvichemicals are the new chemical products from wood. Chemical cellulose from wood pulp is the base of many of today's new fabrics. Silvichemicals are used in ceramics, insecticides, linoleum paste, concrete, paint, agricultural chemicals, rubber and asphalt emulsions.

Wood fibers are pressed into fiberboard to use in building and decorating. Or wood can be taken apart as thin flakes. Then it is molded like plastic to make trays and bowls.

Today 80 percent of the tree is used, instead of the 30 percent used when Pinchot began his campaign to save the forests of the United States. The wood waste that was once left in the woods to rot or start forest fires now supplies half the pulpwood we use to make paper.

But still, wood hides many of its mysteries from researchers. Lignin, the mysterious adhesive that holds wood fibers together, is the target of one group of investigators. Another group of researchers is looking into ways to use leaves.

After seeing thousands of cattle starve because snow covered their food and the ranchers were unable to rescue them, a Texas university professor made a recipe for emergency feed. It consists of chipped-up young mesquite shrubs milled to a flour and mixed with molasses. Another experiment holds promise for humans. Chemists took sawdust and water, sulfuric acid and enzymes. Stirred two hours and evaporated, it became sugar—maybe not the kind that goes best on cereal, but a step in that direction!

Progress is being made by technologists who refuse to throw away our natural resources. In a way, the wood wastes have been gotten rid of, but not as they were in the days of sending chips, sawdust, scrap lumber, and shavings up in smoke. This way we can have our cake and eat it too!

7

Unexpected dividends

PAPER AND BOOKS

THE SUMERIANS who lived in Mesopotamia five thousand years ago wrote books on clay tablets. Fortunately there was plenty of storage space in the ancient Near East, because getting rid of those books would have been very difficult.

Clay is almost impossible to get rid of. A tablet can be buried, even in moist ground, for two or three thousand years and still keep its shape. Once it is back in the air, it rehardens so well that indented cuneiform symbols can be brushed firmly to remove bits of sand or salt. If too much salt has formed in the indentations, the tablet can be baked thoroughly. The clay book can be boiled or even dipped in acid, and it will still be as good as the day it was first written.

The Babylonians, who lived in the same area, pressed envelopes around their clay letters. After the message had been written and baked, a complete coating of heavy clay hid the original letter. An exact duplicate of the message inside was written on the outside, on the envelope. The receiver could read the message first and then open the envelope to check the facts written on the letter inside. Sort of a carbon copy, in reverse. A messenger could get in a lot of trouble if the two messages did not match.

As usual, someone came along to improve on a perfectly good product. The Egyptians had discovered a way to use the reeds in the mouth of the Nile River to make a kind of paper, or papyrus, and found it much easier to write on than clay. Perhaps, too, the Egyptians had a waste problem and preferred paper's easy disposability. The papyrus sheets were rolled on wooden sticks so that they could be held easily. Only part of a letter or book was in view at one time. Some writers pasted sheets of papyrus together, making scrolls over 140 feet long.

The ancient Romans were impressed when they found the Egyptians using paper while they were still skinning lambs, calves, and goats to make parchment to write on. One folio, 200 parchment pages, required the skins of twenty-five sheep. A few sheets of parchment sewn together was called a gathering. Several gatherings were sewn together to form a book called a codex, the ancestor of our modern books.

Meanwhile, a Chinese man named Ts'ai Lun made a startling discovery in A.D. 105. As minister of public works for the Emperor Ho-Ti, he was plagued with trying to keep his office records straight while writing on silk with a bamboo pen. Pounding a piece of the inner bark of the mulberry tree one day, Ts'ai Lun discovered that he had made a very nice piece of paper. He ran to show the Emperor what he had invented, but the Emperor was not at all pleased. It seems that no matter what food they were offered, the Emperor's silkworms steadfastly refused to eat anything except the leaves of that same mulberry tree. If Ts'ai Lun wanted paper, he would have to find some other way to make it. The disappointed minister of public works began to think about another problem that plagued him—old rags and torn fishnets. He mixed them all with some hemp. Then he smashed, stirred, and boiled the mixture—and came up with some very good paper.

It took another seven hundred years for the invention of paper to spread as far as the Near East. Crusaders, looking for lightweight souvenirs to take home, carried the paper to the West. A few hundred years after that, Johann Gutenberg got his printing press going. People laughed at him because, since so few people could read, they won-

dered how he would ever get rid of all those books he was printing. But in the middle of the fifteenth century, life was short and dangerous. Even people who could not read were relieved to have a Bible in their homes, if only to look at the pictures. So Gutenberg had more buyers than he had Bibles.

In the New World, the first paper mill was built by William Rittenhouse near Philadelphia in 1690. Now all he had to do was find some rags. The colonists were poor but thrifty. They were wearing their rags. By 1728, everything had been tried for making paper, including "rotten stone." Rotten stone was really asbestos, and was not burnable. That was regrettable, because it made terrible paper. Ads appeared in the newspapers of Boston, Philadelphia, and New York promising "ready money for clean linen rags" and a bonus of $10 to the person who delivered the most rags in the year 1765. Children's books often included a sermon on "being industrious and thrifty" and urged the children to bring two pounds of rags to the printer's to get a free book.

By the time America had declared her independence and a war was to be fought, the paper shortage was really desperate. "Make a Ragbag" became a war slogan. But now people who had been buying woolens and textiles from Britain had even less need than before for a ragbag. Every tattered suit of clothing must last goodness knows how long. Papermakers were declared exempt from the draft. Letters were written on flyleaves torn out of books and even in the margins of book pages. George Washington wrote battle plans on the back of an envelope from Martha!

As the rag shortage continued, more possibilities were tried. Straw, cornhusks, leaves, even garbage, were mashed and beaten. The papermakers groaned, watching the maddening little wasp make what they could not make. It was 1830 before someone discovered what the wasp had known for thousands of years. Paper could be made from cellulose fibers, which are found in all plants. It can be made from cotton plants, rice and wheat straws, cornstalks, certain kinds of trees, and from grasses like hemp, jute, and esparto. Rag paper today is used only for special documents. Most of the paper in this country is made from wood pulp.

Paper was very easy to get rid of—or so it seemed at first. It burns quickly. Even buried, it will eventually disintegrate. But now there is a demand for stronger paper that is resistant to fire, liquid, and acid. Not only is this paper harder to get rid of, but it brings a real problem.

When papermakers discovered that paper could be made from the cellulose of trees, the nation was covered with forests. Another seventy years would come before anyone worried about chopping down trees. Meanwhile, there was not too much demand for paper. People needed just enough to write some letters. There were not yet any stamps or mailboxes and there were fewer than one hundred post offices in the whole country! Only the educated and wealthy could afford to buy books. There were no paper bags in the grocery. The housewife carried her own basket from home. When a child bought several pieces of penny candy, the storekeeper rolled a cornucopia from wastepaper he had saved, and folded down the top to keep the candy from spilling. There were no frozen-food containers, cereal boxes, cake mixes, soap powders, or wrapped-up loaves of bread. Newspapers made of rag paper sold for 6 cents, which was too much for most people to pay.

Now, with the promise of cheaper paper, everything changed. The penny newspaper hit the streets. The first of a long line of ladies' magazines, *Godey's Lady's Book,* was started in 1830. By the time of the Civil War, thousands of paper bags were being manufactured. But decades would pass before anyone thought of replanting the trees that went into making all our paper goods.

Today there are paper dresses, shirts, baby clothes, bathing suits (!), neckties, raincoats, cups, plates, towels. Just one Sunday newspaper, with 128 pages and a readership of a million people, has used up 140 acres of pulpwood timber. Pulpwood timber is the one fifth of a tree used for making paper products. But a forester cannot cut down just one fifth of a tree—the whole tree must be cut down. In 1969, a part of two million trees was turned into paper napkins and facial tissue. Three million trees became paper towels.

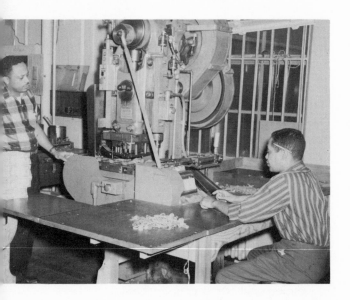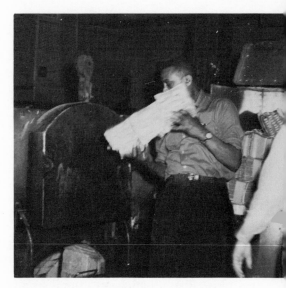

Every day unfit money must be perforated and incinerated

U.S. TREASURY DEPT.

And the pulpwood from four million went down the toilet drain into the sewers!

There are two ways of getting rid of paper, both of them bad. Burning paper pollutes the air, and there are no more places to bury it. But there is a third way! Many times, Scouts or church groups collect old newspapers to make money. They usually have no idea what a favor they are doing. Old paper can be reused to make newsprint (the paper used for making newspapers), or paperboard products like corrugated paper and cartons, or brown kraft paper like that in bags. Every ton of papers collected allows seventeen trees to remain living!

Sometimes paper and books are extra hard to get rid of. Carbon paper, used in offices everywhere, is a problem. It is colored with carbon black, a substance like soot that comes from natural gas. It burns but cannot be repulped because of its oily base. Junk mail makes up much of the heavy load the mailman has to deliver. The law will not allow him to throw it away. It cannot be sent to a person who has moved away because there are not enough stamps on it. It weighs down his bag, but he can't get rid of it. Dead-letter mail is another headache. This includes letters and packages that cannot be delivered because the address is wrong or there is no return address. The person may have moved away, so that he cannot be found. Or the package may be badly wrapped and the address lost. Occasionally dead-letter mail includes material that is not allowed in the mails—matches, fireworks, etc. All dead-letter mail goes to the central post office. There it is

60

opened to see whether the address is inside. If not, it goes on the shelf to be sold at an auction. Magazines are given to local hospitals. Money that cannot be delivered or returned becomes the property of the U.S. Postal Service, which made $100,000 last year!

Recently, vandals broke into a Hebrew school and burned the library. Included in the damaged books were seven Torahs. Each Torah scroll (containing the first five books of Moses) was of parchment. In addition to the actual value of the Torahs, the scrolls are also regarded as very sacred by devout Jews. Talmudic tradition demands that a damaged holy scroll must be buried with dignity and honor, and so a funeral was held before thousands of mourners. The charred remains of the Torahs were placed tenderly in a plain pine box and buried in a cemetery with full honors.

A dollar bill lasts about a year in circulation. A hundred dollar bill may last five years, if it is not stretched too far. Every day twelve million dollars in bills wears out! Worn-out money is sent to a Federal Reserve bank. There the numbers are checked and written down, and the old bills are replaced with new money. When many worn bills are collected, they are strapped into packages of 100 notes each. A canceling machine perforates the packages with several holes. From the time of canceling, the money is kept under the joint security control of at least two people until it is destroyed. The numbers are rechecked and then the bills are burned in a special incinerator installed in the U.S. Treasury Department or the Federal Reserve banks and branches.

Most readers of spy stories know that even charred ashes can reveal secrets. A California man invented the Document Disintegrator after a friend complained that there was no sure way to get rid of top secret documents. The disintegrator is mobile, pulling up at the doors of its customers on a regular schedule. The clients pack their classified and "sensitive" material into large brown bags and seal them: plans for a new automobile to be kept under cover until the day it goes on sale, the design of an airplane that would not fly, checks for thousands of dollars made out to the wrong person, company rec-

Notebooks and pages of secrets enter the disintegrator

DOCUMENT DISINTEGRATION, INC.

61

ords that a rival company might like to get their hands on. When the Document Disintegrator drives up, the bags are fed into the slot. It devours a 12-pound book, three-ring notebooks filled with pages, even computer records fastened together on steel shafts. Forty pounds of secrets turn into a shapeless gray fluff in sixty seconds! A miniature do-it-yourself destructor is available for companies that cannot be reached by the mobile disintegrator.

Libraries find it very difficult to admit that sometimes they really do have to get rid of books. Every year thousands of new books are printed, and thousands must move off the shelves to make room for them. Librarians sell books constantly, or even give them away. But sometimes burning them is the only way. Now a new discovery may make that drastic step unnecessary. Scientists at the University of Denver have found a way to record a thousand pages of the Bible on a film about the size of a 35mm. slide. On a film about three inches square is a library catalog containing 3,000 pages! All the books necessary for four years' high school education can now be packed into a small box.

The wastes that manufacturers once had to get rid of are still surprising researchers. For example, when wood fi-bers are cooked to make paper, an ugly mess called black liquor soap is left in the pot. This black liquid was released into rivers, until pollution experts discovered the waste had a high BOD (Biochemical Oxygen Demand) content. Wastes with high BOD take so much oxygen from the rivers that there is none left for fish or plants. Now that states have been alerted to the seriousness of wastes with high BOD, most states have passed laws restricting the amount of wastes to be released. Paper manufacturers were forced to collect their black liquor in lagoons or else get rid of it somehow. Storing it in lagoons was expensive and involved such problems as killing all the bacteria in the black liquor. Some technologists, working on the other alternative, developed a process to concentrate the black liquid and burn up all its organic content, destroying it and the BOD content completely. This process makes a good weapon against water pollution—but black liquor offers more surprises.

A chemist found that instead of destroying the black liquid he could break it down into several different chemicals. Some industries now turn black liquor waste into the basic ingredients used in paint, varnish, perfume, candy flavoring (anise)—and best of all, the valuable medicines cortisone and ACTH.

8

Landfill and compaction

TRASH

A FAMOUS fictional detective rummages through a suspect's wastebasket. He claims he can learn all there is to know about a person from his trash. Detectives have a lot of trash to work with. New York City discards enough trash in one year to fill fifteen Empire State Buildings. A person traveling around the earth, dropping a hundred tons of trash every mile, would have to make the trip 60 times just to get rid of one year's U.S. trash! Fortunately, there are better ways of getting rid of it.

Some of the world's worst housekeepers lived in an Alabama cave over eight thousand years ago. When they were lucky enough to find fresh food for dinner, they ate everything they could. They even split the bones to get the marrow out of the center. Anything left over was dropped on the floor. When the smell got too bad, it was housecleaning time. The housekeeper brought in a few baskets of clean dirt. Spreading it evenly across the floor, she got rid of the trash and the smell all at once.

Many years later, when medieval Europeans were building Notre Dame in Paris and London Bridge across the Thames, some other early Americans were building the first apartments. These were underneath cliffs in the mesas of Colorado. Not much neater than the Alabama cave dwellers, the Mesa Verde Indians emptied their trash onto a dump that sloped down from their walls into the canyon below. Canyon winds have a way of siphoning the smells down the ravine, so no sensitive noses were offended by the dumps.

The detective who rummages through those wastebaskets is the archaeologist. He can identify the type of civilization by what he "reads" in the trash. Shards, broken pieces of pottery, never decay. Often many pieces of a bowl or jug will be found in the same spot. Decorations on the pottery tell about the artistic ability of the people. Their use of mugs, bowls, and dippers indicates their degree of civilization. Hunters had no time for such niceties. Warrior tribes left behind them arrowheads and spearpoints instead of pottery. They had to eat with their fingers, for they were usually on the move. Farming Indians left behind agricultural tools and sometimes such a variety of plants and animals that even the detectives are surprised at their versatility.

Unfortunately, modern people leave behind too much of their trash. An important part of a city's job is to make sure that the trash gets into the containers instead of on the street. Every trick has been tried, from camouflaging trash-can lids with flower baskets (so people will notice them) to running cartoons such as Vancouver's "Sanitary Sam" in the newspapers. One city has litter barrels painted to look like storybook characters—but it is not the children who litter. Another painted all its trash trucks a pretty daffodil yellow. "Lively Louie" is a New York City trash barrel that has more fun than success. A loudspeaker in the barrel is connected to a microphone hidden in

the bushes nearby. A sanitation squad member, holding the mike, shakes up litterbugs when he shouts, "I saw you! Pick up that candy bar wrapper!"

After the collection trucks gather the trash of a city comes the big problem—what to do with it now. Sometimes it is loaded into trains after being compressed into as small a space as possible. A train may even stop at several other cities to pick up trash or it may run express to a dumping ground miles away. For a reasonable fee a small town can rent a train to haul its trash away. The hard part is finding the place to dump it.

Seacoast towns sometimes dump or burn their trash at sea, although New York City has not used this method since 1934. Flat steel barges loaded with pungent cargo chug out in the morning and drop anchor. When the wind is blowing away from the land, oil is sprinkled over the pile and the fires are lighted. During the thirty hours the trash takes to burn down, the wind may shift often and carry the odors to the towns or beaches. The ashes are brought back and trucked to a dump on shore, because they would not sink before the waves carried them to the beaches.

Beaches have other problems too: broken glass, driftwood, soft-drink cans, and half-sunken ships. Some have sand that will support the weight of a beach sanitizer. But many beaches have sand so soft that the cleaning must be done the expensive way—by hand. Some men earn a living crossing the

A broom to houseclean the city

sands every summer evening with a magnetic detector in hand. It clicks when it passes over something metal—for instance, a lost ring or watch.

Some cities can afford an incinerator, the best way to get rid of trash if it is to be burned. But most cities still burn it in the worst way. It is dumped, along with the garbage, in an open pit. Fires are lit, but they burn slowly because of the wetness of some trash, releasing smoke and fumes into the air.

The trash problems of *Gemini X* were wrapped neatly in plastic bags and ejected into space. But back on land, a ticker-tape parade for astronaut John Glenn was buried in a shower of 3,474 tons of paper confetti and streamers. Two hundred trucks, one hundred mechanical brooms, fifty flushing trucks, and three leaf collectors spent all night cleaning it up.

The method most often used for getting rid of trash is eight thousand years old, learned from the early housekeepers in that Alabama cave. Engineers today call it sanitary landfill.

To select a sanitary landfill site, a community uses many specialists. A geologist makes certain that heavy rains will not carry any pollution through porous rocks into nearby water supplies. Engineers determine whether there will be enough soil to cover over the trash, because the depth of cover is a most important feature. The trash must be buried immediately. The site should be easily reached on good roads in all sorts of weather by the trash trucks from the city. Often, though, the

Shopping carts add to the trash in the Merrimack River

hardest role is filled by the public relations expert. It is he who must convince the nearby residents that the sanitary landfill will not be like the smoking city dump they remember from the old days.

Trash trucks dump their loads of trash on the ground. Tractor shovels push it into a compact pile, squeezing out air spaces. Bulldozers blanket it with earth quickly so that there is no chance for rats and flies to move in.

One 70-foot-long machine can do the entire job almost alone. Rubbish is piled onto an apron and the monster tosses it into his mouth, never to be seen again! Inside, the load is compressed against a knife that lops off chunks. These are shoved downward to the discharge chute. Out through the underside of the machine come 36-inch squares, which then drop into a trench prepared by a trencher wheel while all

65

Paper scrap is sucked into a pneumatic tube, baled, and loaded onto a truck in seconds

CONTAINER CORPORATION OF AMERICA

cials were always afraid someone would get hurt falling into the quarry. Town officials, on the other hand, were always worried about how to get rid of their trash. They got together. Now the school has a baseball field where the quarry used to be—before it was filled with trash. Many hundred years from now, archaeologists may have trouble logically explaining sanitary landfill.

It costs more to clean the city than to run the United Nations

CITY OF NEW YORK, DEPT. OF SANITATION

the digestion was going on inside. The machine inches forward, lengthening the trench while at the same time dropping the load. As a final touch it covers up after itself, tamping the dirt down neatly.

One city built a golf course on top of its trash. An Arizona city built a park, complete with rolling hills of trash. A Virginia city had some difficulty finding enough dirt to cover its hills, but solved the problem by digging a hole. Then they filled the hole with water to make a nice lake. In St. Louis, Missouri a school had a dangerous quarry on its grounds. School offi-

But there is not enough land around to use for sanitary landfill much longer. The trick seems to be in finding a way to make the trash into as small a package as possible. This means squashing

66

it together very tightly, or compacting it, and for this the Shark was designed. New York City bought the Shark for an experiment. Not only will the machine chew ordinary trash; it also grinds up old bedsprings and easy chairs as well. Of course, it has drawbacks. It is too big to go down narrow streets. It cannot move while eating. And the noise while it chomps on an old refrigerator is deafening.

Factories have huge piles of trash that take up valuable space and are a fire hazard too. A machine called a baler solves this industrial headache. All sorts of scrap—fiberboard, textiles, cotton hulls, aluminum, straw, cardboard containers—can be fed into the feed shoot. The waste is then compressed by a ram and exits from the other end all wrapped up in a tight package the size of a washing machine.

On the twelfth day of Christmas, trash men usually wish they were somewhere else. Most ordinary trash trucks will cart away about 50 old Christmas trees. But the new compacter trucks can cram almost 1000 trees inside before emptying out their loads into a landfill. Many of the larger Christmas trees are used on beaches. The sand piles up around the dried-out trees, making dunes for the summer crowds to enjoy. New York's famous Rockefeller Center tree is always cut into several sections and delivered to a mill to be chopped into log-size pieces. The logs are sent to Boy and Girl Scout camps for special campfires.

The most valuable trash in the world

is not even in the world. It is floating around it—in orbit! There was always a little dust out there, raised from the earth by air currents. There are some cosmic ray fragments too, and some cosmic dust caused by meteors. The explosions from the surface of the sun might even have scattered some atomic nuclei around, carried by the solar wind. But there is a lot more space trash now. Every time the hatch of a space capsule is opened, bits of dust and small trash float out. Astronaut Edward White's heat-reflecting glove, dropped during the first space walk, is up there somewhere. And there are several thousand fragments from upper rocket stages, some satellites that did not work, and some that are still working.

This fragment of an Atlas VI *booster orbited earth 6⅔ times before landing in the Republic of South Africa*

NASA

Radar, which is so sensitive that it can "see" a football 100 miles up, keeps track of the various objects. At the last count, 1,691 man-made objects had been "seen" and about a thousand are still there. Most of the others burned up as they reentered the earth's atmos-

Part of a Gemini V *booster, fished from the sea 450 miles from Cape Kennedy*

phere. But at least fifty items have been returned to NASA (National Aeronautics and Space Administration) by people who picked up strange-looking objects lying on the ground. One famous piece was found in Wisconsin, where two policemen kicked it out of the middle of a street. It turned out to be a 20-pound piece of Russia's *Sputnik IV*. When a Titan rocket destroyed itself recently, it added 339 pieces to the orbiting trash pile. A "Satellite Situation Report" is issued twice a month from NASA, telling how much is still up there.

New trash is invented every day. If only "disposables" were not called disposable! That is a name for something you *can* get rid of. We now have "disposable" sleeping bags, blankets, sheets, pillowcases, underwear, towels, and clothing. In addition, hospitals have added "disposable" surgical gowns, lab coats, bed drapes, hypodermic needles, garments for patients in surgery, and thermometers. But the ultimate is the disposable hospital room. With the need for a supersterile room for organ transplant patients, there is now a plastic balloon that can be blown up inside a hospital room to provide a completely sterile environment. All these items are added to the heaps of trash.

Trash can become treasure if we can learn to live with it before we are buried by it. For instance, an incinerator must have a trap to catch the fly ash that used to pour out the chimney and pollute the air. This same fly ash can be sold to use in mixing concrete. But recent tests in the U.S. Bureau of Mines

Wet fly ash, from the incinerator smokestack, contains gold and silver

laboratories revealed that gold and silver from discarded household items such as photographic film and jewelry are also present in ordinary fly ash. The next step for modern science is to learn some way to separate these valuable metals from the residue. Even the waste heat that carries the fly ash out of the chimney can be used. In Long Island, waste heat generates steam to run a plant to desalt water. In Switzerland, the waste heat from one city incinerator heats two hospitals, a dental institute, and a school.

Imagine opening a large cold-storage room to find it full of paper, leaves, glass, tin cans, bits of metal, garbage, upholstery, plaster, stoves, and refrigerators! That is what a laboratory in Cleveland collected as part of a govern-

Bricks made from garbage, leaves, upholstery, plaster, and a stove or two

ment project to turn trash into treasure. The lab shredded the refuse that had been collected from thirty different sections of the city. They added it to fly ash, river-bottom dredgings, waste lime, and sewage sludge. The recipe makes a very fine cake that looks and feels just like a brick. The bricks are so solid after being compacted that when they are soaked in water they actually harden more. Tests are being made now to see whether any pollutants are released when the bricks are soaked in water for weeks. The U.S. Department of Health, Education, and Welfare wants to be certain the bricks will not contribute to the pollution that already affects Lake Erie. If all goes well, the bricks will be made about the size of a suitcase and be used to fill in lands now under water. The bricks may even be used as fill for a "jet port" that will be built offshore in the lake near Cleveland.

Separating the valuables in fly ash from the junk

69

9

Polluted air and water

FACTORY WASTES

INDUSTRIES have various ways of leaving their marks on the world, particularly in the ways they get rid of their waste materials.

All industries have wastes that they must get rid of—to prevent explosions, fires, disease, accidents, smells, and complaints! Many companies use incineration or sewage facilities to dispose of unwanted waste. But many more have problems that are peculiar to their own types of waste. Some industries spend thousands of dollars to find the best method of getting rid of their refuse. Others simply filter it out into the wind, let it seep back in the soil, trickle or pour it into streams and lakes, pump it into the earth, or truck it to landfill areas to be buried. Wherever industries put their wastes, the traces may still be there thousands of years from now.

A pottery workshop on one of the Hebrides Islands had the same problem that plagues industries today—what to do with the trash. Not a single word was ever written about the workshop. The people living there in 1500 B.C.

The Calumet River is heated by steel plants, adding clouds of steam to the smoke

left no writing. Yet archaeologists read this story: The island was warmed by the Gulf Stream and cooled by the rains from nearby Britain. There busy people turned out an unusually high quality of Western Neolithic pottery. The workshop had a horizontal kiln built of stone slabs. The kiln was packed with turf to make it gastight and was covered with a heavy stone slab roof when in use. Birch and willow were used as fuels. Clay, not found on that island, had been transported from other islands. So the potters must have been skilled in making dugout boats as well as in trading and getting along with neighboring islanders. The clay was tempered by a coarse grit, still found along the lakeshore, that had to be ground down by heavy stone pounders. The smoothing and burnishing tools might have been worked by the women, but it took men to lift the heavy stone slabs that roofed the kiln. Trading was good. Matching potsherds have been found on many neighboring islands. From the handprints barely visible on the potsherds, we know the pottery was handmade. But we also know the craftsmen used a turntable, because the decorations follow horizontal grooves too accurate for the steadiest human hand to have made without help. Archaeologists know all this about a people who could not write —because the workshop rubbish heap is still there three thousand years later!

Industries in this country cannot continue another ten years using the same rubbish heaps and systems of disposal they are using now. They need to use water, and so do people. They need to use air, and so do people.

The problem of industry and water is not new. Many early people knew where to mine copper and silver, but until the Romans came along, with their knowledge of transporting water by aqueducts to where it was needed in the mines, very little successful mining was done. A Roman writer, Strabo, says the Romans remelted the Greek slag piles where the trash was dumped at the mines of Laurion, near Athens, and found 33 percent was pure silver!

The problem of industry and air is not new either. The ancient Hebrews ordered that tanneries should be built only downwind of town, and that the threshing floor of a mill must be outside the town because of the chaff and dust.

Blood, paunch manure, and grease add color to a Nebraska stream

The first law regulating sulfurous fumes from coal smoke was passed in 1306. But the first complaint had been received in the eleventh century or thereabouts, when coal had taken the place of charcoal in many industries. One to two hundred years of complaining seems to be about the average before getting action.

Nor are complaining citizens and neighbors the only problem of industries. They have many more. Some of the headaches are brand new, brought about by new materials that do unexpected things—for example, detergents. Some of the problems are old, such as trying to find new uses for what used to be considered waste. Some problems manufacturers learn to cope with, such as getting rid of hog toenails or ditching 10,000 gallons of an ugly shade of paint. Some problems industries try hard to prevent, such as the accidental pushing of a wrong button that sent thousands of gallons of deadly cyanide into a river.

A meat-packing plant has an unusual amount of disagreeable wastes to get rid of. Providing food for the table began as a simple act. A man shot a deer and dragged it home. Providing meat today requires a huge complex: stockyards, a slaughtering plant, a processing or smoking plant, a packing plant, rendering facilities, and refrigeration equipment.

The stockyards use straw and wood shavings in the pen to soak up the worst of the manure and urine. Water runs constantly through the drinking troughs, and hogs must be constantly showered during the hot summer. The underfoot mess goes off to the city sewage plant after some of the manure is filtered out. The slaughtering plant is worse. There the animal's head is removed and the blood drained out. Blood is dried and sold. Beef blood is used for plywood glue. Sometimes dried blood is used in gardens to discourage wild animals from eating the seedlings. The hides of all except hogs are stripped off and sent to the tanner. Each carcass is washed in 50 gallons of water. The hearts, kidneys, brains, and tongues are sold as food. After the contents of the paunch are emptied into the sewer, the stomach is sold to eat as tripe. Intestines and windpipes are washed and used as casings for sausage. The inedible parts are hashed or sliced, then ground up and sent to the rendering plant to be turned into grease or tallow for making candles and soap. Hogs require a special dehairing machine, and the hair can be used for brushes. "We use everything but the oink," is a favorite saying of the meat packer.

Let's consider the hides that went to the tanner. Clothes may make the man today, but in Paleolithic times, a man's new fur clothes were a problem. Soon after his wife put the finishing touches to them, putrefaction (rotting) started. The hair-bearing outer skin, or epidermis, began to separate from the dermis. Quick scraping was necessary before the skin was damaged. In a dry climate, the raw hide would putrify very slowly. The only treatment was tanning, which at first meant rubbing the fat and brains into the leather until it was thoroughly penetrated. A later improvement came when tannin was discovered in the galls of the dwarf-oak tree. Today's leather industry plans its patterns so that almost every inch of leather is used. Small pieces become trimmings, bindings, ornamentation, and buttons. Leftovers can be ground up and used to make leatherboard. Scraps can be used as fertilizer—one gardener even claims to have the only roses in the world raised on mink scraps!

One of the most serious waste problems of all comes from the dairy products industry. There disposal has an extremely high **BOD** content (Biochemical Oxygen Demand). This means that dairy wastes as well as other wastes having a high **BOD** content, demand too much oxygen from the water that they are dumped into. In fact, they demand the same oxygen that the fish and plants need. Yet, dairy wastes are full of nitrogen and phosphorus. There should be some way to make use of those valuable minerals in farming. One of the early dairy wastes was whey, the liquid left over after making cheese. Because it was considered waste and therefore was very cheap, whey was an important part of the peasant's diet in medieval days, probably the only healthful food he had to eat. Not many people buy whey today, but it is there disguised in bread, processed cheese, sherbet, and candy.

It is used to enrich baby formula.

The discovery of a New World with new foods in it did much for appetites. But the chocolate, cocoa, tea, and coffee that had tasted so good in the new countries left something to be desired when they were tried back home. Could it be the honey and unfermented grape juice used for sweetening? Old World cooks decided to use sugar, like the natives in the New World, and so the sugar industry began expanding. Piles of crushed sugar cane remained behind for every little white bag of sugar that was shipped away. To get out the last of the sugar, a great many rinses had been needed. The wet scrap cane, or bagasse, was useless as well as unburnable, until someone discovered that it could be used to make building materials and paper.

The temptation to get rid of the waste from commercial fishing vessels before the boat is back in port is evidently too hard to resist. Ice, brine, water, fish slime, scales, blood, and oil are usually pumped overboard when no one is looking. Near a harbor, the mess clings to pilings and pleasure boats. The slime and blood remain in suspension, while the solids and scales sink. Meanwhile, fish fillets are packed and frozen in neat packages, but the inedible insides, the gurry, are sent to a reduction plant to be turned into fish meal.

As we saw in Chapter 1, the automobile industry can cope with its trash problems—except for one item: tires! Tires burn with such a choking black smoke that even incinerators refuse them. One third of the hopeless tires are sent to a reclaim mill where they become rubber floor mats. But the other 70 percent won't sink, cannot be buried, and will not rot. There are just so many football teams needing tires for spring training. Sometimes old tires hold down the tarpaulins on roadside salt piles. Tires make good bumpers for sharp turns at auto racetracks or alongside boat docks. Tugboats use them as cushions to bump against ocean liners. In St. Petersburg, Florida, two or three tires together, held under water by cement, provide shelters to encourage fish to raise families. That uses up maybe another 5 percent. Someone had better solve this problem quickly!

Food canning creates a great deal of waste that can be surprisingly hard to get rid of. Bits, peels, leaves, stems, and trimmings flow out of the fruit-canning plant in a flume of water. Some material is dehydrated and sold for animal food. Pear waste mixed with finely chopped alfalfa will keep a cow happy. Baby-food makers sell their apple peels and cores to manufacturers of vinegar and pectin. Fruit pits are sold to makers of abrasives like sandpaper. But sanitary landfill, the usual solution for problem wastes, cannot take fruits. Fruit is too wet and requires years to stabilize—that is, to reach the point where it becomes solid and odorless. Because it is wet, fruit also does not incinerate well. Not many alternatives remain for the fruit canner. His waste

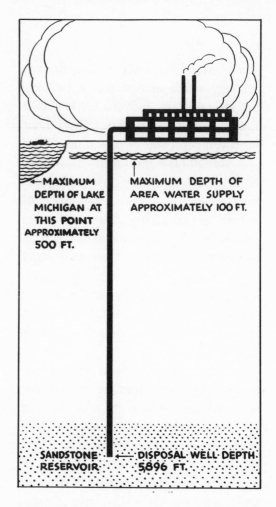

A chemical company makes sure its disposal will not enter vital water supplies
CHEMETRON CORP.

could be fed to animals, but it has the disadvantage of being seasonal. About the time the cows get used to having apple trash for dinner, the end of the apple season comes. Result: discontented cows. Some canners mix their fruit wastes with sawdust and rice hulls and use it for composting, or enriching soil. The mix may not be odorless, but at least it is being useful.

One company must have the prettiest waste in the world. It manufactures colors for makers of paints, inks, plastics, textiles, and other products. Since the colors are produced by chemical processes, the company also has many types of waste materials—gaseous, liquid, and solid. Some way was needed to get rid of the huge volume of water wastes. So a well was drilled over a mile deep that ends in a sandstone reservoir. Thirty-six thousand gallons of waste a day pour into the world's deepest wastebasket.

Steam electric power plants have a lot of excess steam to get rid of. Cooling towers are very expensive and use so much water that a serious water shortage could result. So one power plant faced a choice—either to let the steam off into the air or sneak it into a stream. If the steam was released into the air, people could see just who was adding to pollution. Releasing the steam into flowing water was less obvious. But the hot steam raised the water temperature to 140° F., and everything living in the water died. New uses should be found for steam instead of letting it escape. But what? Chemical engineers recently suggested using the steam to melt ice jams in rivers.

A fine china factory has a unique problem that does not bother many industries. Its products are so well known and perfect that its good name cannot be spoiled by allowing a single imperfect piece to leave the factory. Some factories solve this problem by marking SECOND or IMPERFECT on the article and selling it at a reduced price. But

not the Wedgwood people. They hire one man whose full-time job is to smash every imperfect product. (Off the job, his wife will not even allow him to wash the dishes!)

No matter how carefully industries try to manage their disposal problems, accidents will happen. Probably the stickiest day in history was in December, 1968, when a steel storage tank suddenly burst in upper New York State. Out poured 900,000 gallons of molasses! A workman drowned in the flood when he was hit by a piece of flying steel as the tank exploded. Automobiles stuck on the road. Before anyone had time to find shovels, the temperature began to drop, since it was late on a midwinter afternoon. As soon as the molasses froze hard, the clean-up team said, they would chop it up and haul it away. But the molasses

Not a Christmas tree, but the drilling rig of world's deepest wastebasket
CHEMETRON CORP.

75

never did get hard; it just got stickier. To push it all into the Hudson River would have been easy, but no one could be found who was quite sure whether or not molasses would pollute the river seriously. After the last of the mess had finally been shoveled into trucks and taken to a landfill dump, the molasses company learned two things: First, if they had shoveled the molasses into the river, it would have been as serious as releasing the untreated wastes of over 25 million people. Second, a molasses flood had occurred years before on the Boston waterfront. That day, fireboats had pumped salt water from the harbor over the molasses and emulsified it so that it ran easily. (Try it in a glass.)

Perhaps no industry in the world has more trouble getting rid of its waste than the oil industry. Researchers keep coming up with new ways to use the waste all the time—over 3,000 ways, so far—as well as ways to get rid of the useless waste.

One of the earliest recorded uses of bitumen, from which we get petroleum, was when Noah built his ark. He caulked the seams with pitch. The mother of Moses used it too, so her baby's cradle would float safely to where Pharaoh's daughter came down to the river. The Mesopotamians used it to waterproof their leaky homes. However, petroleum was often found seeping through tiny fissures in solid rock and the escaping gas sometimes made a hissing sound. At least one Egyptian pharaoh is recorded as having consulted this "oracle" just before going into a battle. So petroleum was suspected of being a device of the gods of the underworld. To make matters worse, Pliny, a Roman chronicler, advertised that "because of its inflammability, it is quite unfit for use."

About 1750, Americans drilling for salt brine were inclined to agree with Pliny. They were very much annoyed by the oil that kept coming up with the brine. One salt dealer actually put it in bottles and sold it on the side as medicine. No one wanted that stuff when there was plenty of whale oil to light lamps. But whales were getting harder to catch. About 1854, a man named George Henry Bissell bought some oil medicine and decided petroleum might be worth something—but not as medicine. Not being much of a scientist, he hired a railroad conductor, Edwin Drake, to drill into the ground for oil. In two months the oil boom had begun!

Refining the crude oil into kerosene was a lengthy process. The part that was first vaporized and condensed was a useless liquid called gasoline. It exploded violently when put in a kerosene lamp and lighted. It was difficult to store and dangerous to keep around, so most of it was poured into streams. But within twenty years, researchers had begun to find the first of thousands of uses for petroleum by-products. Some could be used for stoves and to light locomotive headlights. Some removed the lanolin from wool, thinned paints, and were used in making varnish, lacquer, and oilcloth. Paraffin was needed to make candles and to cover the housewives' jars of home-canned foods. Oil and grease lubricated horse-drawn trolleys and factory engines.

When gas and electric lights arrived, the petroleum industry's future looked doubtful. Housewives threw away their old hard-to-clean kerosene lanterns. Something called a horseless carriage had been invented that ran on gasoline, but in all the country there were only a few thousand of them. But the future was doubtful for only a very short while!

Many industries do not try as hard as the oil industry to get rid of their wastes without causing pollution. For example, oil tankers occasionally need a bath. The tanks, as well as the ballast water, get gummy with oil. But crews are permitted to wash out and pump the waste overboard only in certain areas, usually 50 miles out to sea. Some

A close-up of the sprayers in action

THE LAMP, STANDARD OIL CO.
(NEW JERSEY)

oil companies have forbidden their ships to do even that now. They know that a better way of housecleaning must be found, now that the giant super-tankers are coming. The oil industry's laboratories have spent years trying to perfect ways of cleaning up spilled oil. But like all industries, the oil industry has its share of accidents. These usually turn into colossal messes, with much resulting publicity.

An oil sludge lagoon suddenly developed a leak and poured 3,000 gallons of oil sludge into the Allegheny River. Clinging together in a mass twelve miles long, the sludge rode along on top of the river to a dam. Pouring over the spillway, the sludge churned into a huge mass of foam. Health Department Paul Reveres telephoned every town and industry along the river's path, warning each to shut off the water intakes for the next thirty

Laying a detergentlike spray, a boat cuts a path through oil-covered water

THE LAMP, STANDARD OIL CO.
(NEW JERSEY)

hours while the oil passed by. Each time it rode over another dam, the foam piled up high again—all the way to the Ohio River, on the way to the Mississippi.

In March of 1967, a supertanker, the *Torrey Canyon,* split open on a reef and spilled 850,000 barrels of oil into the sea between Britain and France. Nothing like this had ever happened before on such a giant scale. No one knew where to begin. Detergents had emulsified oily messes in the laboratory, so a concentrated detergent was sprayed over the oil slick as it spread out, reaching toward the beaches. Miles of sand in both countries were covered with oil and oily dead wildlife. Months later a sad truth was learned. The detergents had been even more deadly to the wildlife than the oil.

Scientists knew that such accidents were certain to happen again. They redoubled their efforts to find a chemical that could get rid of oil without killing every fish and bird it touched. Less than two years later, a new chemical, developed by a petroleum laboratory, was to get its first test.

At the site of an offshore oil well, the oil had suddenly detoured on its way up to the surface of the Pacific Ocean. A shaft had been drilled over half a mile below the ocean bottom into the pool of oil. A metal casing descended from the drilling platform through 200 feet of water and another 40 feet down into the shaft where the oil was supposed to come up. But the oil found a shortcut through a fault line where the earth's surface had been cracked by an earthquake under the sea. Just before the oil reached the shaft it was supposed to come up, it detoured along the fault and burbled up to the top of the water—beside the shaft!

Everyone was furious—the citizens of nearby towns who watched the beach turning black with oil and the wildlife drowning from the oil coating; the Department of Fish and Game that worked night and day, scrubbing sea birds, fish, porpoises, and seals, to remove the deadly oil; and the oil company that could do nothing quickly to

The rollers of an oil retriever clean up Baltimore harbor

78

Floating boom contains oil spilled after a tugboat hit an oil pipeline in Louisiana

stop the escaping oil. The oil company that had developed the new chemical waited impatiently for permission to try it. But tempers were hot and the permission was not given until almost too late.

At last the new chemical was loaded onto helicopters and boats. The detergentlike spray worked best where there was action in the water, in this case supplied by the churning of the boats and by the downdraft from the helicopter rotors. The oil broke up into tiny droplets, being emulsified much like the molasses in salt water. But too much oil had already worked its way to shore. Straw was sprinkled in shallow water and the sticky mess was raked into piles to be carted away and burned. Eventually the 800-square-mile oil slick disappeared, leaving behind a loud argument over whose fault it was and how it can be prevented from happening again.

These are only a few of the thousands of industries in this country, all with problems that are different and yet, somehow, very much alike. They are all learning that people will make a lot of noise over something they feel is important—like their water and air. They are also learning that they cannot afford to stay in business without finding ways to use many things over again. Getting rid of their wastes is only temporary, until uses are found for them all.

10

Fertilizer and fermentation

GARBAGE

ONLY ARCHAEOLOGISTS really like garbage dumps, and they stick to the ancient ones. Nothing makes an archaeologist so happy as finding something that used to be living. Recently an old corncob turned up in a New Mexico cave. History books had said there was corn here when Columbus dropped anchor in the New World. But until this scrawny corncob proved to be 5,605 years old, no historian would have dared to state that agriculture had that much of a head start.

Possibly the oldest garbage found in this country was in a Utah cave. There were small pads of matted bulrush fibers, chewed to remove the starchy juices and spat out when the flavor was gone. Here was chewing gum over 10,000 years old!

Every living thing has a radioactive kind of carbon in it called carbon 14. As soon as the living thing dies—that is, when a branch is broken from a tree or when an ear of corn is picked—the carbon begins to "decay." It gives off beta particles at a very slow and steady rate. In almost 6,000 years, only half

of the radioactivity will be gone. Therefore, by measuring the number of beta particles given off in a minute, the date when the object was a living, growing thing can be set accurately to within a few hundred years.

In addition to age, the archaeologist can tell the weather and climate of the time from the bones of rats and mice several hundred years old. Occasionally the skeleton of a human being turns up in the garbage dump too and proves that tooth decay, arthritis, and fractures are not just modern problems. The fact that a human being was buried alongside the garbage may not be as heartless as it appears. After all, prehistoric cave beds were made of decaying vegetation. And the action of the bacteria as the garbage heated and decomposed might well have made the dump the most comfortable place around.

During the Dark Ages in Europe, garbage disposal was an uncomplicated matter. The garbage was tossed out of the nearest window. However, in some cities, if a person hit a passerby with the garbage, he was legally liable, as well as liable to a punch in the nose. Sometimes laws required the garbage tosser to shout a warning first.

Garbage tossed into the streets or outside the city gates became nature's problem. A hard rain might wash some away—at least it would go down to the paupers' district. Unfortunately, nature's way of stabilizing garbage is very slow. A rock is stable, because it is chemically inactive. A potato is not. Aerobic bacteria work on it, eventually breaking it down until it is as stable as the rock. But if there is no oxygen present, as in a closed jar or plastic bag, the anaerobic bacteria work on the potato. They putrify it, and it gives off a very bad-smelling gas.

This bacterial action should take place as far from homes as possible. Every city keeps its fleet of garbage trucks in top condition, repairing them during the night because they cannot be spared during the day. Closed trucks are used now instead of the old-fashioned open "salad wagons" that were covered with flies. Housewives always knew when those wagons were in the vicinity—a whiff of the air told them! In Tokyo, garbage wagons play music boxes to warn cooks of their approach. Some cities use closed bins to hold garbage until the truck arrives. Each truck is equipped with a hydraulic lift that raises the bin, upends it so that the garbage dumps into the truck, and sets the bin down again—all without any exposure to the air.

On off days, the garbage trucks are

Refuse trucks compact garbage and trash to take up less space

CITY OF NEW YORK, DEPT. OF SANITATION

used to clean up leaves, plow snow, or spread ashes on icy roads. Large ships often dump garbage overboard when at sea. Result: in their wakes a parade of shark fins.

Private garbage services take care of restaurants and institutions, since their loads alone would be enough to swamp most city services.

The ingenuity of the garbage collector is constantly being tested. In the hot summer months, candy and chewing gum become a sticky and stinging mess. The stinging part comes when the collector and thousands of honey bees compete with each other for possession of the sugary garbage. One collector who has a candy manufacturer as a regular customer oils the inside of his truck just as a baker would grease a cake pan—to keep the load from sticking.

Having a sawdust producer on a list of clients is no fun either. Sawdust can be highly explosive, so no company wants to keep it around long. But it cannot be shoveled into trucks, because the slightest current of air would send sawdust all over. So the collector divides his truck into compartments in order to increase the suction when he attachs a vacuum hose to each compartment in turn.

One of the most expensive items to collect is broken glass. Almost every garbage collector will have at least one company with a great deal of broken glass to get rid of. Tossing bottles into the truck is definitely not the solution. To begin with, glass is much heavier than it appears to be, and the truck's chassis may sag. Glass splinters have a way of working into the truck's compacting machinery, causing very expensive repairs. And removing the

Only the tall smokestacks give away the city incinerator

fragments of glass is dangerous and difficult.

When one collector agreed to pick up chicken and turkey feathers from a poultry farm along his route one December, he thought he was about to make some easy money. The feathers were to be already loaded into barrels when he came for them. But he learned that feathers can weigh like lead, because the defeathering process makes them very wet. He had holes drilled in the barrels to let out some of the water, but they were still heavy. Finally the compaction truck scrunched all the feathers into a tight package, squeezing out as much water as possible. But before the driver had reached the dump, the temperature had dropped below zero and his load was frozen solid! He had to thaw it out by applying a hot high-pressure steam bath to the sides of the truck.

Many homes grind their own garbage in automatic sink disposals, sending the mess off to become the sewage plant's problem. Supersize grinders for city use have been tried, but they require so much water that their loads often overtax the limited sewage facilities.

Incineration of garbage involves problems, since it is usually juicy. Wet things do not burn well by themselves, so some cities compress their garbage and trash together for burning. The garbage truck enters the incinerator plant and passes over a scale that weighs the load. Backing up to the concrete storage pit, the truck empties

Large bitefuls of mixed garbage and trash drop into the furnace

ABINGTON TOWNSHIP DEPT. OF PUBLIC WORKS

its load. Overhead cranes dip into the refuse, picking up large bitefuls and dropping them into the hoppers that feed the furnaces through metal chutes. Incinerators built within the last twenty years are filled and stirred mechanically, while the old-type furnace had to be tended by men using long-handled metal rakes. The burning refuse gradually advances toward the discharge end of the furnace and drops into a concrete tub of water. After the refuse cools, the water is drained off and the residue is dropped into waiting trucks to be hauled to landfill areas directly or by way of barges waiting on the waterfront. About 12 percent of the original pile of trash remains to be buried.

Most cities, however, handle their garbage and trash just as they did fifty years ago. It is dumped into an open pit and burned. Smoke and fumes pollute the air. Rainwater drains down through the half-burned rubbish and pollutes any nearby streams or wells into which it flows. The dump smells horrible, and the rats and flies love it.

Many cities used to allow pigs to roam freely and nibble the garbage in the streets. But now the law requires that garbage be cooked before it is fed to pigs. This is to prevent trichinosis, a disease that is incurable in humans but hardly bothers the pigs at all. The disease is rare in Europe, where pigs have always enjoyed a good cooked meal.

Every person throws away one to three pounds of garbage every day. No wonder the Department of Health, Education, and Welfare is worried. If we cannot get rid of all this garbage, we will have to find some way to live with it.

Sanitary landfill covers the burned refuse. Later this may become a park or golf course

CITY OF NEW YORK, DEPT. OF SANITATION

Burned refuse travels to a landfill site by barge

Europeans use garbage for fertilizer. The garbage is collected and decomposed by microbial action. This means letting aerobic bacteria work on it for three or four weeks. But by wetting it down and turning it over mechanically to let the air get through, the action can be speeded up to four or five days.

In Japan, where there are more people per square foot of space than in most countries, garbage and trash is compacted into small, tight squares. The packages are wrapped in a wire-mesh vinyl so that there is no odor or leakage. They can be stacked on top of each other to fill in low land. Or they can be coated with iron and welded together to make strong building foundations. Or they can be taken out to sea and sunk, even in salt water.

In the future, each home may have to buy its own trash compressor. About the size of a dishwasher, it would dehydrate and disinfect the family's garbage, compressing it into neat little odorless bricks which would then go into the garbage can. The bricks, collected by the trash men, could be used for sanitary landfill. These compact packages would take up less space and provide a more firm foundation than the present system.

Some cities of the world solve their problem by having more rats than people. This is not at all hard to do: simply leave the lids off the garbage cans. A rat will climb a brick wall, swim miles through sewers or a half mile under water, and gnaw his way through cement, wood, plaster, or even lead, to get at garbage. Each pair of rats will eat 34 pounds of garbage a year and will produce 880 more rats in the same length of time!

Ridding the cities of their garbage has many obstacles. But one of the greatest obstacles is that the decision makers—from the mayor to the garbage collector—have no idea that problems exist in their own town. One community in the San Francisco Bay area has 88 agencies responsible for getting rid of the trash. Each one tries to put it in someone else's backyard at 77 different disposal sites.

No wonder they can't get rid of it!

11

Peril to health

SEWAGE

CIVILIZATIONS all began at the water's edge, because the one element man cannot live without is drinking water. And the one thing that can spoil his water is sewage.

Five thousand years have passed since the Babylonians first laid down clay drainpipes to carry their sewage out into the river. Within a few hundred years the discovery had spread to other hot countries. A new type of city was built along the Indus River, which flows from Tibet to the Arabian Sea. Flat-roofed houses, built of brick, faced on paved streets. Indoor wells and bathrooms were standard equipment. Waste water poured from the houses to the streets in closed brick-lined pits. The sewage system was so well designed that for the next two thousand years none could even equal it. No place could have been more sanitary—except for one small detail. The test for good drinking water was "how clear it looks." Traders entered the city one day, about 1500 B.C. Groups of skeletons lay in the streets. The traders wasted no time hunting about for clues to the tragedy. In fact, they left town so fast that no one even remembered the town's name. It is called now Mohenjo-Daro—the place of the dead.

If any people were experts on cleanliness, it was the Romans. The Romans had liberated some colossal sewers, built by the Etruscans, when they entered the city of Rome. Some of the sewers were so large they could be traveled by boat, although this did not come under the heading of pleasure boating. The streets were cleaned every day, and when the traffic got too heavy to clean the streets, the traffic was stopped. For many years, no wheels were allowed in Rome during the day. There were hot baths, cold baths, steam baths, foot baths, and showers. There were also public latrines with constantly running water.

But even the Roman system was not perfect. Soap, as we think of it, was unheard of. The Roman used oil to clean his body. Stubborn grease stains received the oil plus bran-sand-ashes-pumice-and-plant-juice treatment. But no matter how clean-smelling they managed to make themselves, when their clothes were soiled, clean Romans had a problem. Dirty clothes went to the fuller's shop, where cleaning was done with a mixture of fuller's earth (a hydrated aluminum silicate good for removing grease) and stale urine. Even though the Romans had beautiful sewers, the more thrifty citizens, and those who could not afford to pay at the public toilets, saved their jars of urine to sell to the fuller.

Suddenly the Romans discovered they too had the makings of a disaster in their drinking water. About A.D. 100 people were told to drink water only from earthenware pipes, because lead had been found harmful to the human body. Housewives were to test their water by three methods. First the housewife sprinkled some water over a good bronze vessel. It should leave no trace. Then she boiled the water in a copper vessel, cooled it, and poured it off to see if sand or mud lay in the bottom. The housewife could be sure the water was pure if it did not take too long to cook her vegetables. Meanwhile, Roman water-filtration plants purified water by exposing it to the sun and air. Then it was filtered through wool or percolated through layers of sand, much as we purify water today. As an added precaution, they put in drops of wine. Sometimes many drops.

These same sanitation-happy Romans had a shock coming when they invaded Greece. The Greeks were educated and philosophical. Their architecture had reached its peak. But when it came to sanitation, the Greeks had only one word for that . . .

The word was *"Exito!"* and it was shouted out of the window for the benefit of passing Greeks. It meant "Look out below!" and was followed quickly by a bucketful of the day's sewage. After the Roman invaders arrived, the Greek housewife did not bother to shout the word *"Exito"* before throwing. After all, the Roman soldiers did not understand Greek. They understood the bucketful, however, and passed strict laws that ended the Greek system of sewage removal forever.

After the decline of Rome, all the knowledge accumulated by man from two thousand years of sanitation was mysteriously lost. European villages were planned with narrow, winding streets because it was well known that germs traveled up wide, drafty streets. Londoners were ordered to clean the fronts of their houses every week. But the housecleaning chores included unloading their garbage and chamberpot refuse on the dung heap at the edge of town. Drinking water came from wells in low ground. Rainwater drained through the dungheaps and trickled into the low wells. Streets were cleaned only where a stream could be turned so that it would run through the streets and then out into the river. When sewage collected in the few sewers, the farmers used it to fertilize their vegetables. The rivers floated with the garbage of those who lived closer to the river than to the dungheap.

By 1348, disaster could wait no longer. The Black Death killed one out of every four people in Europe! Yet it was forty more years before the British were ordered to stop throwing sewage and garbage into the rivers and streets. News traveled slowly. Twenty years after that, the French king gave the same order.

Four hundred years later, people had completely forgotten the Black Death. There had been few improvements. Versailles Palace had elegant fountains, but the people could not get water to drink without paying for it. A French writer, Stendhal, finally wrote that the streets had been turned into sewers. "It's *under* the streets that sewers should be laid," he proclaimed.

So sewers went under the streets. The smell was ten times worse. By 1800, people were sure that diphtheria and a dozen other diseases were caused by "bad smells." The city of London closed up the holes where the smell was escaping and were rewarded with a series of explosions from sewer gas. A few cities tried capturing the sewer gas to light their streetlamps. Many piped sewage into the fields for fertilizer. In the New World, meanwhile, there was no problem at all. The American colonies had such nice big rivers.

Now that those big rivers are beginning to smell suspicious, people are starting to ask where their sewage goes after it leaves home. Domestic sewage —that is, vegetable refuse, toilet flushings, food, and waste from laundries, bathtubs, sinks, and dishwashers—

flows out of the house through small pipes to larger lateral sewers under the street. Two or more laterals flow together to form a branch, or submain. The main sewer, or trunk, collects sewage from the branches and drains it into the outfall sewer to be carried to the treatment plant.

The engineer who plans sewers for a town has many problems. He uses a map that shows him where every hill and valley is in town, because he must count on gravity to make the water flow. Pumps are used only if absolutely necessary, because they are expensive, and they break down. He checks the area for ridges, four-lane highways, streams, and large rocky areas. He must be careful to build the sewer below the level of people's cellars and yet not bump into curbs, manholes, elec-

A municipal sewer empties into the Missouri River in Kansas

FEDERAL WATER POLLUTION
CONTROL ADMINISTRATION

Aeration tanks expose sewage to beneficial bacteria

ABINGTON TOWNSHIP DEPT. OF PUBLIC WORKS

trical lines, water mains, gas mains, underground telephone lines, or storm sewers. What kind of street paving there is, how wide the streets are, where the house property lines run, and what type of soil he must dig in, are only a few of the things he considers. He dreams of working in a city where the sewers will be built first—then the houses.

When the sewers are built and the sewage pours through them to the treatment plant, the problems are not yet over. A large rainstorm may flood the sewers with the water from the streets. This runoff gets worse as more streets, driveways, parking lots, and school playgrounds are paved and the ground can no longer soak up the water. To make matters worse, the runoff may contain poisons from insecticides and other pollutants, so it must also go to

the treatment plant. A real storm can make the treatment plant tanks overflow, allowing much of the sewage to escape before it is treated at all.

Treatment begins by removing the floating sticks, branches, leaves, and grit from the sewage. Grit may include sand and metal pieces, broken glass, and pieces of pottery. Next air is added to the sewage to make it bubble. As it froths, the oil and grease rise to the top where they can be skimmed off. Then the sewage is sent into the clarifier, or settling tank, where the heavy solids settle down at the bottom, like the mud and sand in the Roman housewife's copper pot. Only there is much more of it. What sinks to the bottom of the clarifier is called sludge. Sludge is removed carefully to keep from stirring it up again.

Sludge is often dried out and used

in cake form for fertilizer. Sometimes it is hauled out to sea and dumped overboard. Or it may be compacted very tightly, squeezing out every drop of water, and be used to fill holes in the land. When it is dried out thoroughly, sewage sludge has enough fuel value to burn. In Paris and Tokyo, burning sludge gives off steam that in turn produces electricity.

Meanwhile, back at the clarifier, the water that is left has received a new status. It is called effluent from now on. Some cities pour the effluent into the nearest river after it has had primary treatment. Actually, the disposal of effluent depends on how loudly the people downstream complain. If they drink the water from the river, they usually complain. Sometimes the effluent is used for irrigation, although not on vegetables that are eaten raw, like car-

rots or celery. Or the effluent is pumped back down into the ground in the hopes that by the time it rejoins the ground waters and comes back up in people's wells it will somehow be purified.

Early explorers talked a lot about the tempting fish in the rivers of the New World. Henry Hudson said there were whales, sturgeon, and shellfish where New York harbor is today. Now, instead of whales and sturgeon, New York's two rivers are filled with one third of the city's sewage.

Any fisherman can tell whether a river is polluted. When the trout, perch, whitefish, bass, and bluegills stop biting, it may not be because of his home-made flies, the special knots he ties them on with, or the kind of bait he is using. Fish just don't stay around after their food supply of tiny organisms and plant life has disappeared. Carp, buf-

Sludge forms in the bottom of the secondary settling tanks
ABINGTON TOWNSHIP DEPT. OF PUBLIC WORKS

89

The end of a favorite fishing spot in Wisconsin

falo fish, and suckers—called trash fish —are not so particular, but one day they too disappear. The river bottom creatures can diet happily on the sludge that blankets the river bottom without worrying about being eaten themselves. But one day even the stone fly nymphs, mayfly naiads, and caddis fly larvae move out. The water thickens, and soon the blackfly larvae, sow bugs, snails, fingernail clams, dragonfly nymphs, and midges have left too. Now the sludges, bloodworms, and leeches own the whole river—if the pollution doesn't get any worse.

Many industries give their sewage the same treatment that domestic or home sewage receives. Often industries have no idea how dangerous their own sewage really is. One night, fire fighters in a New York forest were shocked to discover that a fire was getting much worse even though they were pumping water hard from a nearby stream. Then they discovered the water was full of oil. The river is now legally declared a fire hazard. In another area, a river is used to cool hot steel. The mill detours the water through its plant and releases it again farther downstream. But by then it is too hot for any living thing to survive in it—140° Fahrenheit. Many other rivers and streams have been taken over by blue-green algae. The water is "too thick to swim through and too thin to plant seeds in."

Accidents often happen. One cotton-field owner has his fields chemically sprayed by airplane to control insect pests. But one day the spraying was followed by a heavy rainstorm. The chemicals dripped off the plants, poured through rows of cotton and into a stream. The next morning 70,000 fish were floating dead. Even without rain, pesticides can be deadly. One rancher sprayed his sheep on a hill far from a stream. Afterward, a farmhand sprinkled the hose over the ground "just to settle the dust." And two miles downstream, a trout farm lost every fish.

Nature did not give Lake Michigan an outlet at the southern end. There the water behaves like a bathtub with its drain plugged up. Seventy years ago, some Chicago engineers agreed that Lake Michigan would not be a very good place to send the city's sewage. So they forced the Chicago River to flow west toward the Mississippi River instead of east toward the plugged-up bathtub. But some of the country's largest iron and steel plants send their sewage into the lake.

Lake Erie has a different problem. It is so shallow that if you set the Empire State Building in the center of it, the water would cover only 17 of its 102 floors! Because it is so shallow, the natural aging process, eutrophication, is hurried up by the cities and towns along the lakefront, which all dump sewage into it.

One solution to many of these problems would be for cities to demand secondary treatment for their sewage. This would mean following primary treatment by putting back into the effluent all the oxygen that is needed to keep plants and fish healthy. It also includes further settling, or clarifying, and adding a disinfectant—like the Romans' drops of wine.

Another possible solution is suggested by a popular tourist spot. Every summer day hundreds of visitors drive or climb up Pikes Peak. When they get to the top, they need 15,000 gallons of water each day to wash their hands, have a drink, cook their food, and flush their toilets. Getting even 10 gallons up there is not easy. A small sewage plant was designed so that all the water except that used for drinking and cooking could be used over again. For this, scientists tried the reverse osmosis system. Osmosis is what happens when a dilute solution, like fresh water, forces itself through a semipermeable membrane into a more concentrated solution, like sewage water. Reverse osmosis is forcing the process to work the other way around. Pressure is put on the sewage-water side, forcing it through a membrane, which acts like a series of superfine screens, into the fresh-water side.

Astronauts can escape gravity much more easily than they can escape from their own sewage problems. If men are to spend weeks or months in a capsule or living on the moon, the food, air, and water they carry must take up as little space as possible. The only solution is to reuse everything they can. Scientists are working now on a balanced life-support system that will act like a miniature earth cycle—getting rid of body wastes, supplying oxygen, and removing carbon dioxide. The world's smallest sewage treatment plant, at Brooks Air Force Base in Texas, releases pure water in the same

Oily tributaries empty into Cleveland harbor and Lake Erie

FEDERAL WATER POLLUTION
CONTROL ADMINISTRATION

Bad news on a hot summer day in Michigan

amounts that waste water is fed into it, using the reverse osmosis system. When the system has been perfected, it will be built in lightweight material, such as plastic, for use in space. In order to supply oxygen and remove carbon dioxide, the balanced life support system is counting on photosynthesis —nature's own way by which plants breathe man's waste, carbon dioxide, and man breathes the plants' waste, oxygen. Algae can supply enough oxygen for men, but scientists would like to find a plant that could also be eaten, giving it a double use. So far they have tried radishes, carrots, turnips, endive, Chinese cabbage, and even duckweed!

But back on earth, the problem of getting rid of each person's 100 gallons of sewage a day has not been solved. Freezing it does not work. A proposal to pump it out to sea via a giant pipeline into a deep ocean trench eighty miles off the New Jersey coast is being seriously studied by scientists in Philadelphia, Pa. The contents of the "waste line" would include acids, chemicals, industrial detergents, animal and vegetable wastes, sludges, etc. But one of the most interesting aspects of the proposal is that it would empty out the worst wastes of the entire region around Philadelphia, which includes several large industrial cities. As soon as the "waste line" appears successful, several other regions along the Atlantic Coast will want to try it too. But the plan is not suggested as a cure for all problems of disposal. Reuse of wastes should be considered of first importance.

Meanwhile, another group of scientists finds that sewage added to compacted trash can be formed into solid bricks. These could be used for landfill, road-building, or even for filling in land that is now underwater.

Just like the ancient ideas that sounded crazy at first, some of the new ideas will work too. Progress comes when people are not afraid to try unusual ideas that have a sound scientific basis.

12

Radiation and deadly gas

DANGEROUS WASTES

SOME WASTES are just too dangerous to get rid of in the ordinary ways. Unfortunately, enemies do not come labeled DANGER, and the lesson of which wastes are too dangerous must often be learned the hard way.

One of the discoveries that came from World War II was a chemical to control malaria and typhus fever. It was called DDT, because hardly anyone could spell its chemical name—dichloro-diphenyl-trichloro-ethane. When DDT was sprayed or dusted, the results were dramatic. Beetles, bedbugs, lice, and termites disappeared. Flies died in rooms that had been painted months before with a mixture of paint and DDT. Mosquitoes disappeared where large areas had been sprayed. Soon almost every home, camping site, or picnic basket contained a can of DDT. A few minutes after spraying was done, the disagreeable odor would be gone and so would ants, roaches, and other of nature's valuable but unpopular insects.

Several years later, people discovered that unfortunately the DDT itself did not disappear. Although it cannot be seen or smelled, it may live on for ten years, accumulating in the fatty tissues of living bodies. Washed off the vegetation by rains, it trickles downhill into streams and rivers, eventually winding up in lakes or the oceans. There the DDT is assimilated by plank-

Foaming fingers of polluted water in Washington, D.C.

A fish kill on the Scioto River in Ohio

ton, the food of tiny fish. Each time a larger fish adds another of the tiny fish to its diet, the collection of DDT inside the tissues of the fish grows larger. Finally the fish will be eaten by another fish, a bird, or even a person. The fish may be gone, but its collection of DDT remains inside the consumer, adding to the amount of DDT that has already accumulated there.

Lake Michigan fishermen had almost run out of fishing stories a few years ago. It seemed as if the entire lake would soon be stocked with only one kind of fish—the unpopular, rapidly reproducing alewife. A Pacific Coast salmon called the Coho lives mostly on other fish and shows a distinct taste for alewives. So millions of Coho salmon were imported to Lake Michigan. By the summer of 1968, the

experiment showed signs of being even more successful than the fishermen had dreamed. Millions of dollars were spent on new boats and fishing equipment to be ready for the great summer sport ahead. Commercial fishermen worked on their boats with new hope. In April of 1969, the Food and Drug Administration checked the first shipment of commercially caught Coho salmon. The fish were full of DDT, thanks to the Coho's great appetite for other fish and DDT's "collecting" ability.

Another pesticide investigation was ordered at once by the Department of Health, Education, and Welfare. But it will be months before people can be told exactly how much DDT is safe to consume and what effects the pesticide will have on the human body.

Cities cannot stop pollution from factories outside their limits

Some radioactive wastes are mixed with cement and pumped 1000 feet down

Concrete vaults on the way to burial

Tests being made for Project Salt Vault

A mobile shielded transporter lowers its cargo gently

OAK RIDGE NATIONAL LABORATORY

A herd of sheep demonstrated the dangers of another kind of waste. A few years ago the pilot of a small airplane looked admiringly down at the peaceful scene below him. He saw thousands of sheep grazing on the rolling hills. To be sure, there was not much grass down there, but there were no fences and the sheep could roam miles in their search for food. Not a person was in sight. No wolves, no roads, not even a cloud in the sky. The next morning the sheep lay dead.

What happened? Had they discovered a patch of poison weed large enough to kill six thousand of them? That hardly seemed possible. A check with the local weather bureau told of no storms, no sudden changes in the weather. It was cold and windy, but the sheep had on winter coats. There were a few patches of snow here and there. Sheep liked to eat snow. Was there a chance that a cloud filled with radiation had dropped fallout on the snow?

Finally suspicion fell on an Army testing ground for chemical and biological weapons. A new nerve chemical had been sprayed from an airplane, but it had been very close to the ground. And some of the chemical had been burned in an open pit. But that had been 27 miles away from where the sheep were eating their last meal! The Army paid for the sheep. But people's minds were filled with thoughts of what might have happened.

The people remembered about the sheep, in 1969, when more nerve chemicals had to be gotten rid of. The plan was to railroad the lethal chemicals across the country to a dock in New Jersey. There the cargo would be loaded onto ships, taken out to sea, and sunk. Every state and city the train would pass through stated its objections, and the people won. But the dangerous chemical must be gotten rid of somehow—and so far no one has thought of a better way.

At one Army chemical site near Denver, Colorado, geologists really thought they had the problem licked.

They had found a 12,000-foot-deep well that opened, like a throat, into an underground "hollow" stomach about twenty miles long. Probing scientists and instruments made certain that no underground unseen river flowed through the reservoir. They checked carefully for any undiscovered opening where the dangerous wastes might leak out. It looked too good to be true! Cautiously, in March, 1962, they began pumping poisonous chemical wastes down the well. Then they poured more confidently. Four million gallons later, the earth gave a giant burp. Denver felt its first earthquake in eighty years.

"Just a coincidence," said the Army engineers, as they kept on pumping the wastes.

After four years of "coincidences" like that, the citizens of Denver got angry. But by now the patient was really sick. Three of the largest earthquakes happened a year after the pumping stopped. Should they pump all the chemical waste out again?

"Yes, immediately!" said the residents.

Some rapid calculations by Army engineers showed that they could pump it all out again, at the rate of 300 gallons a day—and that it would take 1,488 years!

In the search for ways to get rid of dangerous chemicals, new ideas come and go.

Wastes could be incinerated, but only if there were some way to prevent dangerous gases from being released into the air. The Department of Health, Education, and Welfare is even concerned about what happens when a farmer collects and burns piles of harvested plants that have been sprayed with pesticides. Does the poison blow in smoke to the nearest town or work down into the ground to come up in next year's crop?

Sometimes dangerous chemicals are dumped into the nearest river. The industry calls this "diluting the chemicals." The neighbors call it "polluting the river." The results may run anywhere from coloring the water harmlessly to releasing deadly poisons. A plant that puts chromium on automobile trim or copper bottoms on cooking pans must rinse its product constantly. All traces of one solution must be completely cleaned off before putting on the next solution. This process is called swilling, and the water from it, the swill, is either sent to the sewage plant or poured into the river. Either way could be disastrous, because the swill contains deadly cyanide. The waste from a large photographic laboratory can increase the minerals in a stream enough to kill all life in it. Even the sun can create poison when it decomposes certain chemicals to the point where they release cyanide.

But dangerous chemicals are not the only wastes in the too-dangerous category. For instance, there are X-rays.

Wilhelm Roentgen was passing an electric current through a tube in his laboratory one day when he noticed some coated paper glowing a greenish-

Lake Erie loses its appeal to fishermen
ASHTABULA STAR-BEACON

blue color. He realized that some sort of rays must be passing between the tube and paper, but they were certainly not very strong rays. They passed through light materials only.

So when the first X-ray machines were built, the notion persisted that these were not very strong rays. They could hardly be considered dangerous when they did not even pass very well through glass. But at a medical convention, when doctors began comparing notes on the wonders of the new machine, the conversation got around to comparing notes on their own few sores and skin conditions that seemed not to be healing quickly. They began to wonder: Could X-rays really be dangerous? Wires were insulated thickly and lead shields were enclosed in the machines. Doctors and dentists were more careful in their use of the X-ray, but still there were no regulations.

97

In New York, a fire and explosion in a nuclear fuel plant, as well as a few radiation "incidents," alerted the city to the dangers in its midst. The Mayor ordered a census and strict inspection of all the X-ray machines, fluoroscopes, and radiographic units in the city. When over 20,000 machines were inspected in 1963, almost two thirds had serious defects. One of the most common defects had to do with the shape of the X-ray beam. A round beam of X-rays used to take photographs on a rectangular piece of film exposed the patient's body to many more rays than were necessary.

Not long ago most shoe stores had fluoroscope machines. Children and their parents could look at the child's foot inside a new pair of shoes and see how much space the growing bones would have. The children had fun wiggling their toes and seeing their bones move on the fluoroscope screen. But not everything fun is safe. Public health agencies prohibited the machines because of the large amount of radiation and unknown harm children could receive.

Most cities now have a set of regulations for owners of fluoroscopes, X-ray therapy machines, and radiographic units. The machines must be inspected regularly by the Department of Public Health. Even a microscopic-size crack would allow a dangerous number of X-rays to escape. Some dentists or doctors subscribe to a monitoring service that measures the amount of radiation each person working in an office is exposed to. Or the dentist may measure radiation himself by carrying a small piece of film in his pocket with a paper clip attached. If at the end of the day there is a "picture" showing where the paper clip rested against the film, X-rays are escaping.

When X-rays are taken, even of something as tiny as a tooth, the nurse always leaves the room. This is because the human body collects radiation—just as it can collect DDT. The nurse and the doctor or dentist are using the X-ray machine many times a day, and they would very quickly collect too much radiation if they stayed with the patient. The patient, on the other hand, uses the machine only a few times a year, so he is in no danger at all.

All the successes and mistakes in getting rid of dangerous wastes have been only practice for getting rid of the most dangerous wastes of all—the radioactive ones.

There are over nine hundred radioisotopes from a hundred chemical elements. They cannot be seen, heard, smelled, tasted, or touched. They are so dangerous that they can affect a person's unborn children or grandchildren. They may be liquids, solids, gases, or even dust. They may dissolve easily, or they may not dissolve at all. They may give off different types of radiation at different energy levels. Some of the rays, like alpha particles, can be blocked by an ordinary piece of writing paper. On the other hand, some—like gamma rays—can penetrate through several feet of concrete.

Radioactive waste can be burned, buried, sunk in the ocean, added to other chemicals, blown up—anything. But no matter how hard scientists try to get rid of it, there is one indisputable fact about radioactive waste. Each particle of it will decay at its own peculiar rate. Some will decay in a few seconds. Some will take thousands of years. But man can do nothing to hasten the rate of decay.

Since there is no way actually to get rid of radioactive waste, the problems of the U.S. Atomic Energy Commission are centered on storing it safely until it finally decays naturally.

We are surrounded by radioactivity constantly. Radioactive elements are in the ground where we grow our food, in the water we drink, even in ourselves. The job of the Atomic Energy Commission is to keep the level of radioactivity as close as possible to this nat-

Burial sites are selected carefully for their geological characteristics
NUCLEAR ENGINEERING CO., INC.

ural level. But in addition to the natural radiation surrounding us, there are many other sources. Danger or potential health hazards are measured by microcuries. One microcurie is one millionth of a curie. Low-level radioactive wastes in liquid form have less than a microcurie of radioactivity to a gallon. Intermediate-level wastes may contain anywhere from one millionth of a curie to a full curie of radioactivity to a gallon. The high-level wastes have from several hundred to several thousand curies per gallon.

Low-level radioactivity may be found in the water pumped from a uranium mine in New Mexico. The water is allowed to seep back into the sandy soil and poses no threat. Air from a mine ventilation shaft may contain radon 222 dust, but it is no more harmful than that released by rocks of the earth's crust. Nuclear power plants that generate electric power usually re-

A chemical company buries its own dangerous wastes
DOW CHEMICAL CO., ROCKY FLATS PLANT

lease their low-level radioactive liquid wastes into nearby rivers after diluting them with water.

The real source of radioactivity worry is the high-level wastes. The largest source of these is the irradiation of nuclear fuels in reactors. This process creates a great deal of waste that will be "hot," or radioactive, for a great number of years. This waste must be made as small as possible because the ways for getting rid of it are limited.

When the Atomic Energy Commission looks for ways to get rid of any of its radioactive wastes, there are not too many choices. Gaseous wastes are usually held in tanks until they decay. Then the gas is released into the air. Solid wastes are usually moderately radioactive and are buried. These may include worn-out clothing, glassware, blotting paper, and other debris. Liquid waste is often poured into some absorbent material like vermiculite so that it will be more solid to handle. One atomic energy plant has a disposal tunnel for getting rid of radioactive chemical processing equipment that is too large to bury. The equipment is loaded onto railroad flatcars and shoved into a tunnel almost a half mile long. When the tunnel is full, it will be covered over with earth.

Every year millions of dollars' worth of machinery, equipment, and tools must be buried because they are contaminated by radioactivity. Contamination is not the same as being irradiated, because there is no atomic change taking place to make the machinery radioactive. Just the same, it is "hot" and therefore dangerous. Radioactive "dirt," usually consisting of alpha, beta, or gamma rays, is deposited on the object and must somehow be cleaned off. The cleaning bill for these machines comes to $1,000 a day! This is why, especially for porous surfaces such as cast iron that soak up contaminating matter, it is cheaper to bury a machine than to clean it.

The Atomic Energy Commission gets rid of its high-level wastes by storage. Sometimes the wastes can be stored a short time and then released. Other times the storage is permanent

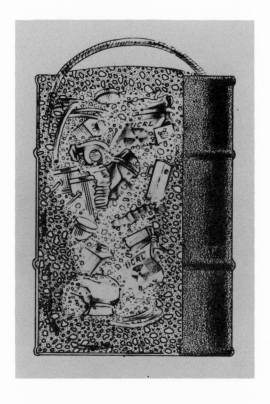

Radioactive waste is embedded in concrete
LAWRENCE RADIATION LABORATORY,
BERKELEY, CALIFORNIA

100

—it will last until the radioactivity in the product decays to a safe level. Sometimes this storage will have to be continued through several generations, so the name "perpetual care" is given to it. Radioactive wastes are stored for one reason: to give them time to decay where they cannot harm people. But all radioisotopes decay at different rates.

The life of a radioisotope is counted by half-lives. One half-life is the time it takes *half* of that radioisotope to cool. For example, strontium 89 has a half-life of 54 days. After that time, it will be half stable—no longer active—and half very much alive. In another 54 days, it will be down to one fourth active and three fourths stable. In another 54 days, it will be one sixteenth lively, and so on. But what about radium 226 with a half-life of 1,622 years? Or carbon 14, which the archaeologist uses to date some of his treasures? Carbon 14 has a half-life of 5,700 years.

Most high-level radioactive wastes are buried alive. They are put into steel-lined reinforced concrete storage tanks or are mixed with concrete and put in steel barrels. Burial grounds are chosen for their geological characteristics and their distance from heavily populated areas. Only the Atomic Energy Commission or private companies licensed by the AEC are responsible for burying the dangerous wastes. But the AEC is beginning to run out of places to use for burial. A recent experiment tested the possibility of using abandoned salt mines. Salt mines are dry and eliminate some of the hazards of groundwater, which might flow through the wastes, leaching out some of the radioactivity and carrying it to areas where it could contact humans. In addition, salt has an ability to change shape under pressure and could close up by itself if any fracture, such as that caused by an earthquake, should rupture the walls. Project Salt Vault is a series of tests to learn whether the salt mines could be used for some of the radioisotopes that will take hundreds or thousands of years to die.

Radioactive trash may be collected only by licensed companies. These companies have their own disposal sites with earth-moving equipment for quick burial of trenches and concrete-lined wells. The companies must obey strict

Burial trenches must be above the water table

OAK RIDGE NATIONAL LABORATORY

rules for using special containers to keep radiation from escaping. Their tank trailers for carrying radioactive liquids are made of half-inch steel plate and have monitoring devices to detect the slightest leak. The drivers are specially trained in case of accident. They carry decontamination equipment and chemicals, as well as signs and ropes to close off a dangerous area. Even then, they are not allowed to use certain highways or go through the centers of some cities. If the radioactive material is carried by railcars, it must be in concrete vaults, securely fastened down with iron bars and marked DANGER. Felt dipped in asphalt covers the wood floors of train cars.

At the radioactive burial ground, which is surrounded by high fences, the containers are lined up in trenches. Usually each day's load is covered with dirt, but this is not as necessary as it was in sanitary landfill, since this trash is already in special containers. Burial grounds have bin vaults, with one-foot-thick concrete plugs to cover the hole after the drums of "hot" stuff are inserted. Trenches cannot be so deep that they are near groundwater, and they must not be dug in places where rainwater will drain through them, such as on a hillside instead of in a low spot at the foot of the hill.

Each person working in the burial area wears two exposure indicators. One is a film badge such as the dentist uses when taking X-rays. This is clipped to the clothing and developed once a month. The other is a self-reading dosimeter called a pocket-ionization chamber. The employee looks into a small window at one end to see how much radiation he has been exposed to so far that day. Every night when he goes home, the amount is recorded in a book and the dosimeter set back to zero. The employee may not even wear home the clothing he has worn all day, but must shower to decontaminate his body and leave his work clothes to be cleaned by a special process. Even the

Bins for solid radioactive waste storage have foot-thick concrete plugs

ARGONNE NATIONAL LABORATORY

102

water that pours over him and his clothes is contaminated. Some of the jobs at the burial area require special clothing, breathing devices, and other safety equipment.

With so much attention paid to controlling radiation, it is surprising that any ever has a chance to escape. But it can. The water that cools the nuclear reactor often carries away contamination—sometimes as much as 50 percent of the contaminants are still in it. Sewage effluent can contain radioactivity and be dangerous if it is used for irrigation. One city is thinking of exposing its sewage to massive doses of radiation to kill the germs and then piping the sewage far away to get rid of it. It could be less dangerous to keep the septic sewage.

The Atomic Energy Commission spends much time and research making sure the water and wildlife around atomic energy plants are not being affected by radiation. Radioactive tracers are allowed to escape and are followed to find out where radiation might collect.

The four thousand industries that make and use nuclear products are just a beginning. Eventually all industry may be running on nuclear energy. Now is the time to be careful. The Atomic Energy Commission wants to be sure to lock the barn doors *before* the horse gets out!

BIOGRAPHY OF SUZANNE HILTON

SUZANNE HILTON uses any excuse she can think of to find adventure and enjoy nature.

Born in Pittsburgh, Pennsylvania, she was five when her parents drove the family to California in a 1927 automobile. Not all the roads were paved. Maps were rare and inaccurate. And motels had not even been invented. She attended nearly a dozen public schools before studying at Pennsylvania College for Women (now Chatham College) in Pittsburgh, and graduating from Beaver College, in Glenside, Pennsylvania.

During World War II she used her knowledge of languages as a volunteer in the Foreign Inquiry Department of the American Red Cross. After the war she married Warren M. Hilton, now an industrial and insurance engineer and Lt. Colonel, U.S. Army Reserve.

The Hiltons began camping when their son was eighteen months old. Their daughter was only six weeks old the first time she slept in the woods. The family car has lumbered thousands of miles, piled high with the gear of Cub Scouts, Boy Scouts, Brownies, Girl Scouts, and foreign exchange students. The family now spends weekends and vacations in their sailboat, dropping anchor most often in the coves of Chesapeake Bay.

"But something happens to nature lovers when they find pollution spoiling their country," Mrs. Hilton says. "It is impossible to be an American without loving nature. American history is colorful with rough natural beauty, explorations, and adventures in the wilderness."

A free-lance writer, Mrs. Hilton has found her latest adventures in libraries, at local waste disposal plants, and in checking facts on pollution with various technologists.

BIBLIOGRAPHY

The following were used for reference, covering subjects in several chapters:

Encyclopaedia Britannica, 25 vols.

Forbes, R. J., *Studies in Ancient Technology,* Vols. I–IV. Leiden: Firma E. J. Brill, 1965.

The New York Times, articles, 1968–1969.

Singer, Charles, and Underwood, E. A., *A Short History of Medicine.* Oxford University Press, Inc., 1962.

Singer, Charles, *et al.* (eds.), *A History of Technology,* 5 vols. Oxford: At the Clarendon Press, 1954–1957.

Stewart, George, *Not So Rich as You Think.* Houghton Mifflin Company, 1968.

World Book Encyclopedia, 20 vols.

The following provided background material, and the newspapers and magazines provided up-to-date information for each chapter:

Chapter 1 AUTOMOBILES

American City, "Successful Attack on the Auto Blight," Feb., 1968.

Architectural Forum, "Drop City—New Life for Junked Cars," Sept., 1967.

Business Week, "Car Junkyards Try Sophistication," Feb. 26, 1966; "The Plastic Car," May 4, 1968.

Chemical Engineering, "Junk Cars Up-grading Ore," May 9, 1966.

Engineering, "Valuable Scrap from Valueless Cars," May 13, 1966; "Scrap Turns to Iron Powder," May 10, 1968.

Engineering News-Record, "Build with Junked Automobiles," May 23, 1968; "Autos and Cities Don't Mix Well," May 30, 1968.

Iron Age, "Junk Cars," March 4, 1965; "The Poor Man's Shredder," April 22, 1965; "Scrap Processing Goes Big Time," Aug. 26, 1965.

Machine Design, "The Staggering Scrap Spectacle," July 7, 1966.

Modern Tire Dealer, "What's to Become of Scrap Tires?" May, 1968.

Product Engineering, "Can Engineering Cope with the Debris of Affluence?" Oct. 9, 1967.

Public Works, "Junkyards Are Necessary," Dec., 1966; "Today's Pride and Joy; Tomorrow's Refuse Problem," Jan., 1967; "Junkyard Screening—Nevada," March, 1967.

Steel, "Ford to Use Junk Autos for Foundry Scrap," Dec. 20, 1965; "The Ford Fragmentizer," Jan. 24, 1966; "Low-grade Taconite Upgraded with Scrap Steel," Aug. 1, 1966; "Shredders," Dec. 12, 1966.

Wealth Out of Waste, Pamphlet, U.S. Department of the Interior, Bureau of Mines Programs in Solid Waste Utilization, no date.

Chapter 2 PLANES AND TRAINS

Air University Review, "Aeronautical Geriatrics," Col. I. R. Perkin, no date.

Aviation Week and Space Technology, March 7, 1966.

Business Week, "Where Ghosts Come Back to Life," June 17, 1967.

Desert Bonanza, Pamphlet, Military Aircraft Storage and Disposition Center, Davis-Monthan Air Force Base, Arizona, no date.

National Geographic, "Fun Helped Them Fight," Jan., 1948; "Aviation Looks Ahead," Dec., 1953; "History Written in Skies," Aug., 1957.

Chapter 3 SHIPS

Dugan, James, *The Great Iron Ship.* Harper & Brothers, 1953.

Engineering News, "Old Freighters to Form Breakwater," Nov. 18, 1965; "If You Can't Refloat a Wreck, Bury Her," Aug. 18, 1966.

Marine Engineering/Log, "Ship Scrapping Count," June 15, 1965; "Ship Scrapping Continues," June 15, 1966; "Ship Break-Up Rate," June 15, 1967; "The World's First 3-D Enlargement," May, 1968; "Ship Scrapping," June 15, 1968.

National Geographic, "Ships Through the Ages," April, 1963.

Newark Star Ledger, "Ship Ahoy at Stevens," Sept. 27, 1967.

Philadelphia Magazine, "The Queen Elizabeth," June, 1968.

Reader's Digest, "New Goliaths of the Sea Lanes," July, 1968.

Shipyard News and Views, "Unique Retirement for a Midbody," July, 1964.

Chapter 4 BUILDINGS

Business Week, "Closing a Hotel at a Profit," July 23, 1966.

Construction Methods, "Air Hammer Works High to Bring Wall Low," May, 1967.

Engineer, "Engineering Aspects of Hemisfair," March–April, 1968.

Engineering News, "World's Fair Postlude," Oct. 21, 1965; "Fair Demolition to Yield Test Data," Dec. 23, 1965; "Stinger Brings Down Walls," Nov. 24, 1966.

Safety Maintenance, "Outmoded Buildings Endanger Lives," July, 1966.

The Saturday Evening Post, "He Gets Paid to Smash Things," Feb. 6, 1954.

Chapter 5 CONTAINERS

Department of Agriculture Yearbook 1966, "Protecting Our Food." U.S. Government Printing Office, Washington, D.C., 1966.

Design of a Water Disposable Glass Packaging Container, Progress Report #1, submitted to U.S. Public Health Service, Solid Wastes Environmental Control Administration, by Samuel F. Hulbert and C. Clifford Fain, April, 1969.

Food Technology, "Packaging Materials—a Lot of Rubbish?" June, 1968; "Frontiers in Packaging," Aug., 1966.

McGraw-Hill Yearbook—Science and Technology, "Food Packaging." McGraw-Hill Book Company, Inc., 1968.

Chapter 6   WOOD

American Forests, "Wood Waste Finds New Uses," June, 1966.

American Paper Industry, "New Pulp Source," Jan., 1965.

Breetveld, Jim, *Treasure of the Timberlands.* Scholastic Publications, in co-operation with Weyerhaeuser Company, 1968.

Journal of Agricultural and Food Chemistry, "Feeding Value in Wood," Nov., 1964.

Life, advertisement of International Paper Company, June 21, 1968.

Parks and Recreation, "Don't Underestimate Wood Chips," April, 1966.

Pulp and Paper, "Wood Utilization; What It Is," May 1, 1967.

Tappi, Technical Association of the Pulp and Paper Industry, "Pulp from Sawmill Wastes," Sept., 1966.

Chapter 7   PAPER AND BOOKS

American Paper Industry, "Deepwell Disposal," Feb., 1966.

National Committee for Paper Stock Conservation, "Old American Institution Brings Nostalgia and Money," Feb. 19, 1968.

Newsweek, "Shredded Secrets," Feb. 28, 1966.

Weeks, L. H., *A History of Paper Manufacturing in the U.S.* New York: Lockwood Trade Journal Co., 1916.

Chapter 8   TRASH

American City, "Refuse Is the Sweetest Fuel," May, 1967; "Solid Waste Research Projects," June, 1967; "Neat Little Bales of Garbage," Sept., 1967; "Storybook Character Litter Barrels," Feb., 1968; "Trash Trains," Aug., 1968.

Baldwin, Gordon C., *America's Buried Past.* G. P. Putnam's Sons, 1962.

The Bulletin, "Junkpile in the Sky," Philadelphia, Nov. 17, 1968.

Engineering News, "Will We Bury Ourselves in Garbage?" May 19, 1966.

Hibben, Frank C., *Digging Up America.* Hill and Wang, Inc., Publishers, 1960.

The Jewish Encyclopedia. Funk & Wagnalls Company, 1904.

National Geographic, "Russell Cave, Alabama," Oct., 1956, and March, 1958; "Mesa Verde," Nov., 1959, and Feb., 1964.

The Philadelphia Inquirer, "The Growing Peril of Pollution: Time to Face the Consequences," July 28, 1968.

Popular Gardening and Living Outdoors, "It's Beautiful; How Do We Get Rid Of It?" Dec., 1967.

Public Works, "Sanitary Landfill Lives Up to Country's Expectations," July, 1965; "Collection Trucks," Aug., 1965; "Operation Big Squeeze," Jan., 1966; "Gravel Pit to Landfill to Park," Feb., 1966; "Oversized Burnable Wastes," April, 1966; "Revamped Refuse Dump," Jan., 1967; "How to Clean Up the Beach," May, 1967.

Refuse Collection and Disposal. U.S. Department of Health, Education, and Welfare, Public Health Service, Bibliography Series #4, Supplements B, C, D, E, and F, 1954–1963.

Rock Products, "Gravel Pit to Golf Course," June, 1967.

Sanitary Landfill Facts. U.S. Department of Health, Education, and Welfare, Public Health Services Solid Wastes Program, Cincinnati, 1968. Publication #1792.

Sanitation Industry Yearbook. New York: Solid Wastes Management, 1969.

Solid Waste Handling in Metropolitan Areas. U.S. Department of Health, Education, and Welfare, Public Health Service, reprinted 1966.

Summaries of Research & Training Grants in Solid Waste Disposal. U.S. Department of Health, Education, and Welfare, Public Health Services Solid Wastes Program, Cincinnati, 1967.

Chapter 9   FACTORY WASTES

American City, "Are Litterbugs Getting the Word?" July, 1967.

Bottom-Dwelling Macrofauna in Water Pollution Investigations. U.S. Department of Health, Education, and Welfare, Public Health Services Environmental Health Series, Cincinnati, 1966. Publication #999–WP–38.

Focus on Clean Water. Federal Water Pollution Control Administration, revised 1966.

Gurnham, C. Fred, *Industrial Wastewater Control (Chemical Technology,* Vol. II). Academic Press, Inc., 1965.

Lipsett, Charles H., *Industrial Wastes and Salvage.* Atlas Publishing Company, 1963.

A Look at Our Water. Federal Water Pollution Control Administration, a reprint of the Jan. 1966 issue of *Talmanac,* house magazine for Talman Federal Savings and Loan Association, Chicago.

Marine Engineering/Log, "Cleaning Tankers," Feb., 1965.

A New Era for America's Waters. U.S. Department of the Interior, Federal Water Pollution Control Administration, reprinted March, 1967.

Public Works, "Waste Disposal for Ford Motor Plant," May, 1968.

Science News, "World's Deepest Wastebasket," April 16, 1966; "The Army's Colorado Waste Disposal," May 4, 1968.

Chapter 10   GARBAGE

Business Week, "Garbage for Health and Power," July 1, 1967.

Engineering News, "Composting Gets Rid of Garbage," April 28, 1966; "Will We Bury Ourselves in Garbage?" May 19, 1966.

Machine Design, "The Great Garbage Explosion," Feb. 3, 1966.

The Sun, "Garbage: Paying the High Cost of Affluence," Baltimore, Nov. 24, 1968.

Chapter 11   SEWAGE

American City, "Worldwide Rush to Incineration," Dec., 1967; "Geophysical Instruments Locate Landfill Sites," May, 1968; "What Good Incineration Means," May, 1968; "Sludge Disposal at Sea," June, 1968.

Carcopino, Jerome, *Daily Life in Ancient Rome.* Yale University Press, 1958.

Dupont Magazine, "Quenching a Worldwide Thirst," Jan.–Feb., 1969.

Hardenbergh and Rodie, *Water Supply and Waste Disposal.* International Textbook Company, 1966.

Information Fact Sheet, "Plant for Space Waste," Aerospace Medical Division, Brooks Air Force Base, Texas, 1966.

Pollution Caused Fish Kills, 8th Annual Report, Federal Water Pollution Control Administration, Washington, D.C., 1967.

Robiquet, Jean, *Daily Life in France Under Napoleon.* The MacMillan Company, 1963.

Schrier, Arnold, and Wallbank, Thomas W., *Living World History.* Scott, Foresman & Company, 1964.

Science Digest, "Sewage Treatment in Space," April, 1967.

Summary Report, Advanced Waste Treatment. Water Pollution Control Research Series, July, 1964–July, 1967; Cincinnati, 1968. Publication #WP–20–AWTR–19.

Technology Week. "Waste Treatment in Space," Jan. 9, 1967.

Chapter 12   DANGEROUS WASTES

Atomic Power Safety. U.S. Atomic Energy Commission, Division of Technical Information Extension, Oak Ridge, Tenn., Dec., 1967.

Chemical and Engineering News, "Known Methods Can Cope with Atomic Wastes," Feb. 28, 1966.

Engineering News, "Chemical Waste Line—10 Miles to Sea," Sept. 8, 1966.

Public Works, "Plating Wastes," May, 1967.

Radiation Control Program of the New York City Department of Health. New York: Office of Radiation Control, June 1, 1965.

Radioactive Wastes. U.S. Atomic Energy Commission, Division of Technical Information Extension, Oak Ridge, Tenn., May, 1967.

Science News, "Atomic Wastes," June 3, 1967; "Sheep Die Near Nerve Gas Tests," April 6, 1968; "Army's Colorado Waste Disposal May Be Causing Earthquakes," May 4, 1968.

Water and Sewage Works, "Wastes from a Photographic Lab," March, 1968.

INDEX